"HE IS REAL!"

~ ~ ~

The Biography of
VERISSA WALBER,
A Great Woman of True Faith

Dr. Luanne Nelson

"He is Real!"
The Biography of Verissa Walber, A Great Woman of True Faith

Author: Dr. Luanne Nelson
Editor: Lyda Rose Haerle
Interior Layout: Griffin Mill
Cover Design: Dr. Luanne Nelson & Michael Nicloy

Paperback ISBN: 978-1-957351-76-6

Hardcover ISBN: 978-1-957351-77-3

Published by Nico 11 Publishing & Design, LLC
Mukwonago, Wisconsin

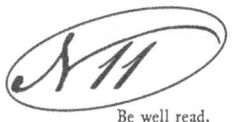
Be well read.

Quantity order requests may be emailed to:
mike@nico11publishing.com

Printed in The United States of America

Jesus Christ is the same yesterday, today, and forever.

Hebrews 13:8

Vickie insists on making sure
every person who reads her story gives
all glory
to our Lord and Savior
Jesus Christ!

"He is Real!"

Preface

How do you thank someone who has saved you from death?

I know I speak for the thousands of men, women, and children who have been touched by this woman of God. She has worked tirelessly since 1980, for over 40 years, to bring the Gospel of forgiveness, service, mercy, love, and salvation to anyone who will listen.

How do we thank her? How do we honor her?

Her life's story is both tragic and miraculous. It truly is a privilege to write about it. She is my teacher, my pastor; I am blessed to call her my friend, my sister.

~~~

When we met, I had walked away from two corrupt churches, was told I could no longer teach at a third, and found myself to be an outcast in another spiritual desert, confused and hurting. There was no place left to go. The big-shot leaders and deep-pocketed benefactors in those churches didn't want me, I was of little use, I was garbage to them.

I was in that lonely desert for two long years. Walking past godless churches, my resolve was strengthened to never step foot into one again.

Four thousand miles away from each other, we connected by cellphone, solely perchance. We ended up talking for over two hours. At the end of our conversation, I shook off every speck of that desert sand; she had loved me back into His service in just over one-hundred-twenty minutes.

You see, her ministry's motto is this: "If nobody else wants them, they are perfect for us!"

She does this for everyone. She knows it's up to the person with whom she's speaking whether or not they will shake off the dust, sand, and dirt of their life. It's completely up to them. Free will. Her job is to show up where He puts her and to tell them about Him no matter what they decide.

As our friendship grew, we saw how our lives overlapped in so many ways, and, as with all of God's children who love Him, it became clear why He put us in each other's life that day, over a decade ago, on purpose for His glory.

Each one of us has something in common, really. We all are a mess in one way or another. We all need a Savior. She led me back to Him.

~ ~ ~

She has started hundreds of missions all over the world; her name is not on one single one of them. "This is not about me," she says emphatically, "It's all for Him and the building of His Kingdom!"

She is propelled by the power of the Holy Spirit; He is her best Friend, her Confidante, her Comforter, her Answerer of all questions.

She is filled with supernatural peace beyond understanding, a wonderful sense of humor, and divine patience; however, brimstone fire will come out of her mouth if she sees you offending her best Friend, putting yourself in peril.

She is hell-bent on you not spending eternity in hell.

~ ~ ~

The blind see. The deaf hear. The lame walk. Twisted spinal columns are straightened in the blink of an eye. Wounds needing stitches close miraculously, skin restored to perfection without any trace of an injury. Declared dead at the scene of an accident, a lifeless driver will gasp a deep breath of air and live, stunning the paramedics. Entire families surrender their lives to Jesus, their Savior. There are countless numbers of miracles. She gives all glory to God each and every time.

"Without Him, we can't do anything; with Him, we can move mountains," she says.

She insists His Holy Spirit will work like this through any willing vessel, through any person who has faith.

She's correct, you know. I know this firsthand.

Why haven't you heard about her? It wasn't time, yet.

It's time now.

*I must work the works of Him who sent Me while it is day;
the night is coming when no one can work.*

John 9:4

Table of Contents

Part Two

Part One

Introduction

You don't know her name, her beautiful face is unrecognizable. I can tell you though, when she walks into a place, her presence pulls all of the air out of it; you have to stand next to her to breathe again.

A store will be empty. No cars. No customers. She'll park her car, walk in and start gathering her goods. By the time she checks out, the store will be filled, a long line behind her waiting to check out. I've been with her and watched this happen time and time again.

People are drawn to her.

Even so, people often treat her badly. She was terribly hurt when she was a child. There was a day she was stuck in the bottom of a well with no one to pull her back up. She was lowered into it by a very mean man. She didn't fear death only because she was too young to know about death. She didn't like how dark it was down there, though, and she was very hungry.

She ran away from that place of her childhood as soon as her legs were strong enough to run far enough, fast enough.

There's a hell on earth that we can fall into, pushed by cruelty. It can trap us, and, for a while, hell had her stuck to its walls.

It is the place we cannot outrun. There's no exit. Strings of days blend together, filled with shots of brandy, glasses of wine, and straight white lines of fairy dust to sniff for a quick, pretend escape. Before you know it, colorful pills, the lucky charms of counterfeit deliverance, dot dresser tops, ready to pop for the next trip to nowhere.

Hell is red-hot, and there are not enough tears on earth to put out that fire.

Hell is very real.

So is Heaven.

Chapter One

God Saw It All

For You formed my inward parts;
You covered me in my mother's womb.
I will praise You, for I am fearfully and wonderfully made;
Marvelous are Your works,
And that my soul knows very well.
My frame was not hidden from You,
When I was made in secret,
And skillfully wrought in the lowest parts of the earth.
Your eyes saw my substance, being yet unformed.
And in Your book they all were written,
The days fashioned for me,
When as yet there were none of them.

Psalm 139:13-16

Deep in the wintertime of 1953, there was a tiny four-year-old living in Minnesota who didn't stand a chance. Her little legs could not outrun the monsters chasing her in her own bedroom – they looked just like her mom and dad. They yelled at her to get out of bed to clean up the kitchen floor. She jumped out of bed, ducking to avoid being smacked, and ran toward the kitchen.

She knew she had no other place to go – even if she could outrun them.

She joined her big sister, already on the floor, wiping up the monster's carnage from the night before.

Shivering from the cold and shaking in fear, she inched her way back in bed next to her sister, her little brother still asleep at her feet. Minnesota nights were freezing, and the threadbare blanket barely covered them. They were glad they had each other to stay warm.

She couldn't sleep, though.

Quietly, her teeny feet tip-toed to the corner of the bedroom where her dolly sat on the floor waiting for her. Her hair was half gone, and she was missing an eye. Little Verissa loved that babydoll despite its brokenness and held it tightly against her chest.

It was a short-lived reverie.

The silence was broken when one of the monsters opened the bedroom door, hollering, "We're going to the bar. Get your clothes on and let's go!"

This time, she remembered to grab a coat and mittens for her little brother. She knew they would be in the car all day long without any heat while their mom and dad went into a building. The children were not allowed to go inside. Little Verissa spent all day in that car, day after day, wondering what went on in there. She knew it had candy bars because her mom would bring a few for them to eat when it was getting dark out. She wanted to go home so they could have some rice and beans from the people who lived downstairs.

She had to go to the bathroom very badly but didn't because she knew if she wet the car seat, she would be beaten.

She thought about her grandma. She wanted to go to her house and color. Grandma always had crayons and cookies. She had a good grandma and a bad grandma. The bad grandma made her sit on the kitchen floor with her big sister and little brother all day and sometimes all night. They weren't allowed to make any noise while the grownups played cards and got drunk in the next room.

Her tender, young life got even worse a few months later.

Verissa's dad found temporary work on a farm that summer with other farmhands. Her family moved into a cottage with a low ceiling next to a big white farmhouse. The floor was cracked, with a big, tattered rug covering it.

There was a wishing well next to the cottage, so she was happy about that – but not for long.

She vividly recalls the day:

> I really did love the little wishing well at the beginning. I would find tiny slugs, or washers, and pretend they were coins. I'd make a wish: I want a family that loves me, I want to live in a big house like my grandma, and always have enough food to eat, and real toys to play with. I'd toss it over my shoulder and into the well and hear it plink somewhere deep down in the hole. I'd peer down into the darkness and whisper I love you and listen for the echo.

> I was doing that one day when daddy and the other farmhands had an afternoon off. He had gathered them around himself and was playing the guitar and singing. Of course, they were drinking beer and getting drunker and drunker. I was pretending not to notice them, but felt the dread creep up my back when I could sense they were walking toward me. Dad shoved me out of the way and put a big watermelon in the bucket of the well and lowered it down into the water until it floated out of the bucket. "There!" he said with a grin, drunken drool squeezing out of the corner of his mouth. That'll keep it cold.

One of the hired hands staggered up and peered down the well. "How are you going to get it back up?" he wondered. Meanwhile, I was slinking away in fear I wanted to be neither seen nor heard. My dad's angry voice stopped me dead. "Don't go anywhere, Verissa!" he ordered.

Fear poured over me. I peered up at him, my eyes asking why, but my voice afraid to speak. "You're how we're going to get the watermelon back up!" The hired hand slapped him on the back. "Great idea!" he slobbered, "What, it'll be cold in about an hour?"

"Yeah," dad turned back to me, "You sit right here by the well until we're ready to get the watermelon out." For the next hour, I sat in the dust, in the skimpy shade of my wishing well... my well that was supposed to make my dreams come true. Now I hated it. I despised my well. It was now my dad's well, for whatever belonged to my dad was poison to me.

Finally, the hour was up, and dad and the hired hands wanted their watermelon. He grabbed me roughly, and with the help of one of the other hired hands, hoisted me into the bucket. It was tippy and I grabbed the rope, fearing I would tip over into the well. They all laughed at me.

"I am so creative," my dad said arrogantly. "You're just the right size!" he guffawed. The others laughed with him. My heart pounded so loudly I was afraid he would hear it. They lowered me down the slimy narrow shaft until the bucket was just below the water level. I felt the cold-water creep up my back and I clung to the rope. "Now get out and put the watermelon in the bucket," dad ordered.

I slipped a couple of times, and the bucket kept tipping, but I finally was able to get out. I cringed as the icy water curled up around my neck. I clung to the bucket with one hand and pushed the watermelon toward the bucket with the other. I kept slipping, and finally had to let go of the bucket in order to use both hands to put the watermelon inside.

Instantly, I was under water. I came up gasping and tried again, dog paddling as hard as I could. After several more attempts, I finally succeeded. As soon as it was inside they quickly hauled up the watermelon, and then sent the bucket back for me. I had a little trouble climbing in but was afraid to ask them to lower the bucket a little more. I finally succeeded and they hauled me up.

It soon became routine to send either me or my little brother down into the well to retrieve their icy watermelon. The well was no longer my friend. It had become a dreaded enemy. I would sit at the steps down into our root cellar cottage, and stare at it in hatred, thinking of ways I could destroy the well.

Then one day, after I successfully retrieved their watermelon, Dad tied off the bucket, and walked off, laughing, leaving me down in the well. "Daddy, no!" I screamed, "Don't leave me down here!" I heard dad shout back at me, "You can swim."

"No!" I screamed and sobbed; dog paddling as hard as I could. There was no answer. I continued to scream and dog paddle as the sun started to go down. I wedged myself against the slimy walls to rest but soon those muscles got tired so I'd go back to dog paddling. I learned how to do the survival float, where I would curl up like a ball and rest, only coming up every 30 seconds or so for air.

The water got colder and colder, and my muscles began to cramp up and get weak. I thought for sure I was going to die. Finally, I spied the bucket coming down toward me. I was going to be saved! I felt my heart leap with hope. It was my mother saving me. It had to be my mother. Surely my mother loved me and wanted me alive.

Many years later I found out it was my sister! She had run away after retrieving me, afraid of punishment. My mom and dad had passed out.[1]

She would survive this and many other horrific moments in her younger days, including being sexually molested by the farmhands in between being lowered into that well, and being struck by a car while running home after doing an errand for her mother when she was in the second grade. She was hurrying because she knew if she took too long to get back home, her mother would beat her.

~~~

The only reprieve this little girl would get would be summers spent at her beloved grandma's house, the one who had pretty coloring books and warm cookies. Verissa remembers her grandma asking her if she'd ever been to church. Of course, the little girl's answer was, "No."

Grandma encouraged her to try to feel God's presence – whatever that meant. Little Verissa clearly remembered her grandma telling her how her great-grandfather was visited by God and healed of many physical afflictions during the Welsh Revival, whatever that was. Asking what an affliction was, her grandma explained, "A sickness or a physical problem."

Little Verissa wondered, "If God is real, why wouldn't He fix her family?" She thought about all the wishes she had made at the wishing well and how, in the end, the well didn't do a thing for her except bring pain and misery. Maybe God could fix things, but she doubted it. She surely wasn't going to risk more pain and misery wishing for anything.

Grandma told her she prayed for her every day. Little Verissa was convinced God wasn't listening anyway even if He was real, but she remembers she wanted Him to listen. She remembers thinking maybe she should just try to believe it even though it seemed pointless.

She recalled how Grandma wanted her to pray with her at night, and she did, even though she didn't feel like asking God to bless her very mean mom and dad. She remembers praying with her grandma just in case God was real. She figured maybe God could fix her dad so he wouldn't be so mean. She wanted to stay at Grandma's house forever. That was not going to happen, though, so back home she went when summer was over.

~ ~ ~

A little while later, her dad moved the family to Washington State and got a job in a restaurant kitchen. He decided to take little Verissa to work with him. She was 9 years old. She learned how to debone a chicken and make radish rosettes in between washing dishes. When the owners gave her money for her work, her dad would take it from her immediately, calling it "rent money."

The next few years were filled with her mom and dad getting her drunk for fun. She doesn't remember much of her early childhood except being sent to her dad's sister's house to milk lots of cows because her uncle was too sick to do it. She was glad she didn't have to go to school because she could not read anyway.

At the tender age of 13, Verissa decided she had had enough. She walked away from her family with the clothes she was wearing and not one other thing. She said goodbye, without regret, to the neighbor's daffodils lining the sidewalk as she walked to the city bus stop, got on a bus, and went downtown to look for work.

She landed a job as a waitress, at the age of 13, after lying about her age. She easily passed as an 18-year-old since she was already six feet tall and fully physically matured. Even though she could not read or write, she remembered what the customers ordered, where they sat, and what they looked like. It was a breeze for her. She slept in the city park until she had enough money to rent a small apartment across from the park.

Her parents never came looking for her, and she never gave them a second thought, until the following year when, after being raped and then falling sick with pneumonia, she was forced to go back home because she was out of money and could not work.

At the age of 15, she left home again, once and for all, landing a job as a riveter for Boeing. That same year, she would meet Celeste.

Celeste and Verissa would forge an alliance of friendship, love, and sisterhood that would span over six decades. They both were runaways, escaping the drunken perversion of their parents, who would rather beat them and sell them for sex than have them sit down with them at their dinner table.

They both were tall, curvy, and beautiful, and quickly realized they could make a lot of money if they worked together as a team.

It wasn't long before they figured out they could make more money as strippers than as waitresses or riveters. They couldn't be molested by the gawkers who were not allowed to touch them as they stripped; they could go home and sleep alone without being groped or raped.

San Francisco beckoned them, so off they went to make their fortune. They picked roadside flowers and put them in their hair on their way. It was the '60s...free love reigned, and they capitalized on it. They were seventeen years old. Finally free from the treachery in their childhood homes, they believed they finally were in control of their own destinies. Their soft hearts had not yet turned into stone.

~~~

You need not be dragged through the details of the miserable things these two beautiful women went through. A lurid timeline of decline will be described herein, instead. The descent into desperate debauchery was not rapid. It spanned a very long time, punctuated with disease and death around them. Celeste and Verissa were brought together as sisters in spirit, they stuck together with a grace they could not see, keeping each other alive during the direst of circumstances.

~~~

Arriving in the City of Love, they were enchanted by the crooked and steep streets of San Francisco. They started stripping at night at the Mission Theater downtown. It was fun at first – and lucrative.

In the sordid, cruel world of stripping, *sexy* turns into *shameless* pretty quickly. This is the place where hearts slowly are hardened.

As always, when we are paying attention, God will send a messenger at just the perfect time. Their first job would have them stripping with a woman who called herself "Joan the Missionary." They had dinner together after stripping one night during their first week of work. We were curious where Joan got her stripper-name.

I [Verissa] asked, "So how did you get the name Joan the Missionary? Is that some sort of play on Joan of Arc?"

Joan smiled. "You're not going to believe this, but when I was about 25, I was swimming in the ocean and got caught in an undertow. I was sure I drowned. In fact, I believe I really was dead, but I called out to Jesus. I don't know how He did it, but suddenly I was out of the undertow, and it spit me up onto the beach. So now I'm stripping for Jesus. That's why I call myself Joan the Missionary. I tell people about Jesus."

I didn't know anything about Jesus, but it seemed kind of weird to me. "Would Jesus want people to take off their clothes and get men turned on?" I questioned myself. I said to Joan, "So what do you tell people about Jesus?"

"I tell them just what I told you – that He saved me from drowning in the ocean."

"Why do you think he did that?" I asked. I thought about how he hadn't saved me from all the pain and abuse of my childhood, and how he didn't save my wonderful aunt from cancer years ago.

Joan answered, "I don't know. But I think I have a higher calling in life. I think I'm supposed to be a ballet dancer. I have been saving all my money in my room so that I can put on a ballet."

Celeste and I looked at her, puzzled. "A ballet...what kind of ballet?" I asked.

"I don't know. A Jesus ballet."

By now we were getting the picture that this girl was just a little off in the head and wished we hadn't gone to dinner with her. She was just too weird.

"By the way, I think we are neighbors," she said. "What's your room number at the mission hotel?"

"Room 315," I replied.

"I'm in room 317 next door. Isn't that something?" Joan said.

Yeah.

I rolled my eyes at Celeste.[2]

~~~

Things did start going bad pretty quickly for the two young stripper-sisters. Back in the 60s, racial rioting overtook San Francisco; it was a dangerous place to live, certainly not conducive to nightclubbing or stripping. Celeste, Verissa, and three other headlining strippers headed for Stockton.

There, they rented a dilapidated upstairs apartment from a woman who invited them to have chicken dinner every Sunday downstairs with her family after they worshiped their Lord Jesus at church.

"There it was again," Verissa thought. "This wonderful lady worshipped a God who didn't appear to do anything for her. All she had in her refrigerator were eggs to eat during the week and a chicken on Sunday, and she was living with cockroaches and termites. What was the point? Maybe He was around for the Welsh revival and then went back to sleep," she reckoned.

They started stripping at the One-Eleven Club, also known as the "Bucket of Blood." It lived up to its name; fights were frequent, and the booze oozed from everyone's pores. Celeste experienced her first drunken night and grew fond of alcohol there. That club was short-lived; Verissa and Celeste were offered their own bar to manage by a skinny man named Melvin who wore horn-rimmed glasses and drove a black Lincoln Continental.

Of course, they said yes. It was a new adventure for them. Melvin was smitten by the two of them. He loaned them his car and gave them a few credit cards after they were banished from the One-Eleven Club for being the centerpieces in an all-out brawl. They drove his car up to the coast, performing impromptu strips along the way and maxing out his credit cards. They called him to tell him his Lincoln was in Seattle.

The two sisters were unforgettable and untouchable, or so they thought.

Chapter Two

"You Are Mine."

Be pleased, O Lord, to deliver me;
O Lord, make haste to help me!
Let them be ashamed and brought to mutual confusion
Who seek to destroy my life;
Let them be driven backward and brought to dishonor
Who wish me evil.

Let them be confounded because of their shame,
Who say to me, "Aha, aha!"

Let all those who seek You rejoice and be glad in You;
Let such as love Your salvation say continually,
"The Lord be magnified!"

Psalm 40:13-16

While in Seattle, they unwittingly became entangled in organized crime and intentionally dabbled in the dark arts. Drugs and alcohol permeated their lives. A certain bitterness moved in and took up residence in their souls. Trapped and abused as children, they realized they had set themselves up for the same abuse as adults.

At 22 years old, Verissa, while at a stripper-bar with Celeste, accidentally drank from a glass of alcohol laced with strychnine that had been meant to kill Celeste. Verissa was locked in a hospital mental ward for what was mistaken as a suicide attempt. Verissa later would star in a motion picture, called *The Fifth Floor*, which showcased her experience while locked up there. Ninety days of confinement, as mandated by the State, brought a living hell to Verissa's life – complete with seizures from the strychnine, shock therapy because she repeatedly denied she was trying to kill herself, and rape by the orderlies as they bathed and showered her at night.

Things got even worse after her release.

Verissa continued stripping in Washington until her organized-crime bossman offered her an opportunity to go to Alaska with Celeste to work in a new bar in Anchorage. In her own words, "Mike sent us to Alaska to open bars for him. I was done just stripping. I wanted my own bar. He had promised that to me for years, but I was no longer sober or drug-free. I had a $1,200-a-day drug habit and drank a gallon of wine before I would even leave my apartment each day. My life of debauchery, and of trying to run away from my past, caught up with me. It had caught up with Celeste as well."

They jumped at the chance to go to Alaska.

In the 27th year of her life, Verissa, who called herself Vickie at this point, found herself in a very dark, cold place, where the only escape was with drugs and alcohol where she became totally immersed in both.

It was a steep, icy slope into an abyss of unhinged perversion.

Men from all over the country were in Alaska working on the pipeline and the oil fields. Money was plentiful, but the men were rougher and tougher. There was no playing. It wasn't long before Vickie was addicted to hardcore drugs – uppers, downers, and everything in between. She needed drugs and alcohol to achieve any semblance of peace.

Celeste took off for Dillingham, Alaska, to bartend – sick and tired of being a stripper. Vickie became housemother to the other strippers. They all took their clothing off together on stage at night; she was their designated protector. She was almost 30 years old.

Vickie considered being a prostitute, figuring it would be easier than stripping.

Ten months later, a very bored Celeste returned from Dillingham, all coked up but no longer drinking alcohol. She considered herself sober from alcohol despite the cocaine addiction.

The sisters were glad to be back together again.

Vickie decided to open up a new bar in Anchorage called The Great Alaska Bush Company. Of course, the best strippers would work there. Vickie also invited girls up from Seattle and California to work at her new place in the new frontier.

The Bush Company became an instant hit; Vickie let it be known she was available as a prostitute for $1,000 a night. She figured prostitution would augment her income enough to keep her addictions afloat.

Organized crime found out about her new nightclub and put a contract out on her life. She knew she didn't really have anything to live for, so it didn't matter to her.

~~~

One day, Vickie decided to go home to visit her mom and dad in Washington. Even though she had been sending money to them whenever they contacted her asking her for some, it had been a long time since she had seen them. Her dad greeted her with a leering grin, congratulating her on being a famous stripper and prostitute. He bragged that she had a reputation he had heard about all the way to Washington State.

She saw the irony in finally being accepted by her dad as a success, even if it was for being a successful whore, and continued sending as much money to her parents as they needed.

One night, after her shift as a stripper was over, Vickie walked to her Mercedes to see a dead cat and a dozen black roses on her car. She drove home to her apartment, not knowing her car had been rigged with explosives. She arrived home safely and collapsed on the couch, exhausted. Her rest was interrupted by a loud banging on her door.

It was an off-duty police officer who yelled to Vickie that her car was on fire and to call the fire department. The firemen and police responded but the Mercedes was destroyed. One of the officers asked Vickie if she was aware there was a bomb in the car. Vickie had no idea and told the officer she had just driven it home. The officer's face blanched as he told her, "The bomb was set up to the ignition. You are one very lucky lady. Do you have any idea who could have done something like this?" Of course...she knew!

In her thirties, Vickie decided it was time to stop stripping altogether and take the easier road of working strictly as a prostitute. There would be no more henchmen ruling over her, no more death threats, no more managing schedules, no more house-mothering other strippers.

In her area of work, Vickie had always tried to avoid married men, and she figured she could do that much easier as a prostitute because it would be easy for her to check her customers for wedding bands or tan lines around wedding-band fingers on the married men she wanted to avoid.

Vickie said of this time: "Celeste and I ended up in Kenai, Alaska, working for a woman with a brothel. We were the best, still. Men would fly in planes full of their buddies to see us. We dated famous people, and we also dated everyday normal people, all the while either drunk or high."

And, Vickie tells of a special event that took place during this time of her life:

> One day, while in town, I saw a flyer about a *revival*, and I wanted to know what the heck it was about. A gal I worked with warned me to stay away from it, which piqued my curiosity even more.
>
> Now, from the flyer, I could tell that the revival had something to do with church and Jesus Christ. All I knew about religion was a little prayer my grandma had taught me. My dad had always mocked anything that had to do with religion and Jesus. To me, the words, "Jesus Christ," were words to be said when angry. In addition, at Eadie's, we would often sit around the television in the evening and watch Christian broadcasts, mocking it just like my dad did.
>
> But then, way back in the fog of childhood memories, there were grandma's words about the Welsh revival – there was that word – *revival*! I vaguely remembered it. I vaguely remembered something about my uncle getting laid out flat by the Holy Spirit and being healed. But the memory was so mixed with drugs and booze, I wasn't even sure it was real anymore. I also remembered my thoughts about how God must be sleeping because He didn't heal my aunt or prevent my awful childhood.
>
> So, we got loaded first, grabbed a cab, and went to the revival. When we got to the big white tent on Funny River Road and walked in, everyone stopped talking as they looked at us. They all knew who, or I should say *what*, we were. We walked right up to the front row and sat down.
>
> The first night of the revival was like any other for me, I was drunk and high. Something weird happened during that meeting...I sobered up. The preacher man kept telling us about some man named Jesus and boom I was sober. It was so incredible.
>
> Still, there was something working at me on the inside, and apparently it was working on all of us, because when the

preacher asked people to stand up and say the sinner's prayer at the end of his preaching, we all stood up.

Of course, I had to do a little urging. "Come on," I whispered to my four friends, "The preacher said to stand up if you're a sinner, and we're sinners. That's us. We need to say the sinner's prayer."

Slowly, the other four stood to their feet. We repeated what the preacher said, "Dear Jesus, I am sorry for the life I've lived...I am sorry for my sin. I repent for it now, and I ask you to forgive me...make me new...make me a new person... change my life...I commit myself to you...I place my life in Your hands. Thank You for coming into my life, thank You for Your forgiveness, thank You for giving me a clean heart in Jesus' name. Amen"

I waited for some kind of wind or light or something to make me different. What I discovered was that I no longer felt high. I'd come into the revival tent loaded, but the revival had stolen my high. At first I was a little miffed. But then I thought about it and decided it was a good thing.

I whispered it to Celeste, "Hey, are you high anymore?"

She thought about it quickly and turned a puzzled face toward me and said, "No, I'm not. That's weird. It must be God."

This happened every night for two weeks. Edie wasn't too happy about it, but we could still make it back in time to make money for the night.

But now, it was not only us five whores, but I also started flying people down from Anchorage. I'd call them up and say, "You've got to hear this guy talk about Jesus. You won't believe it. You go in there drunk and come out sober. You can go in high and come out straight. You won't believe it! It's phenomenal."

I had expected my life to change, but it didn't. So even if it were possible, I became a bigger drunk, a bigger junkie, a bigger pervert. I totally lost what little restraint I previously had.

When I got angry, I'd just grab a gun and start shooting through the windows. I'd go into rages and throw champagne bottles at people. If I wanted to walk naked around the bar, I did. I did whatever I felt like doing. If I had any kind of respect for myself as a person, it was now completely gone.

I'd ask men who came into the bar if they knew anything about Jesus, and they looked at me like I had gone crazy. I wanted to know, to understand, but there was no one to tell me. I was glued to Christian broadcasting. Now, I didn't make fun of it, but I really didn't understand it, either. The changed lives those Christians kept talking about just made me angrier. Mine hadn't changed. What was wrong with me that God didn't like me?

I had no idea what was going on. I didn't realize it was the grace of God. Nobody told me I had to go to church, nobody told me to buy a Bible and read it. I just knew that when I walked in where the man was talking about Jesus, I sobered up.[3]

~~~

Vickie's life got worse after the revival; she was depressed and angry. Then, one evening, everything changed.

Vickie tells the story:

One night I put on a white jumpsuit and sat at the bar, eyeing a group of men who had come in from the oil fields. I knew they were eyeing me. I could tell they were making bets on which one of them would get me for the night. Finally, a man – I found out later his name was David – came up to me and started to say, "Hey, beau…"

I cut him off. "Go f… yourself. You punk, go date one of the ugly girls down there. I don't want anything to do with you." I walked to the other end of the bar, ordered my own white wine, and continued to drink alone.

The other men left, but he stayed. He finally approached me again. "I don't want to have sex with you. I just wanted to buy you a drink. Will you let me?"

I perceived an inner strength I hadn't seen in many men that frequented Eadie's. He wasn't trashy, and he looked cool in his white sweater, so I relented. "OK. Get me another white wine."

He motioned for the waitress, who already knew what I wanted. We had a relaxed evening full of small talk.

"I've been transferred up here from New Mexico," he said. He started to tell me about himself, that he grew up in the Midwest, loved his father, and had been married once for five years. He was a former Marine who had served in Japan.

I opened up a bit, too, telling him a little about my childhood in Minnesota, but staying more to safe things like the fun time I had in San Francisco as a stripper.

He came into the bar every night, just to hang out with me. He didn't pay to sleep with me; he just wanted to get to know me, which was different than other men. I started to warm up to him. He seemed to be a dependable person, secure in who he was, and didn't criticize or gossip about people. I could tell he was a hard worker.

I had always found men to be repulsive, and didn't want to have sex and do all the other perverted things they wanted me to do, but now that I began to have feelings for David, I found it even harder to have sex. That meant I had to get even more loaded and drunk in order to allow a man to approach me. My rages got even more outrageous, and people would hide when they knew I was drunk and on the verge of a rage.

I finally decided I just couldn't do it any longer. I couldn't be a prostitute. Instead, I invited David into my bed.

But having David wasn't good enough either. I didn't quit alcohol or drugs and was as big a junkie as I could become. So even though I now had an actual boyfriend and had quit prostitution, hopelessness and anger at God controlled my life. I hated myself, and I hated God.[4]

Nine months after Vickie had stood and asked God to forgive her at the revival, she walked up the stairs to Room One, her private bedroom at the brothel, and began screaming and cursing, specifically at God.

"You, God! You created mankind. How could you create me to be a whore! How could you allow me to have a father who gave me to his farm hands so they could abuse me? How could you let him whip me constantly for no reason? Why did you let me feel and suffer everything I did? Why didn't you save me like everyone said you would?

I liberally sprinkled all my screaming with vulgar profanity. I picked up my purse and threw it against the wall. "You must have created me to be a whore. Is that what you want? You want me to be a whore? Is that what I'm supposed to be? Is that my lot in life? I hate you! How could you let me be such a thing? I hate myself, and I hate you for giving me the kind of life you gave me so that I had to become a whore. Why did you create me dyslexic? Why did you not let me learn to read? How could you be a loving God, like they all talk about, and let all these things happen to me? What's wrong with me? Why did you give me grand mal seizures? Did you just create me so that I could be humiliated and degraded?

I shook my fist at him, sobbing. I picked up a water glass and smashed it against another wall. The sound carried to the bar room beneath, and all the customers cleared out. Edie was not going to make money this night.

32

I continued my tirade. "You are a fake and a liar! I gave my life to you six months ago. You said you'd change it, and you haven't. I'm not waiting any longer."

Right then, I decided I was going to cheat this fake and liar of a God out of the rest of my life. He thought he was so big, the creator of mankind. I was going to double cross him.

I was in my 30s, and I was going to take my own life so that he could no longer use me as a whore. He could no longer abuse me.

With that decision, I calmed down and sat at my dressing table and carefully put on my makeup. I put on my most beautiful white, floor-length peignoir with its flowing sleeves and hood trimmed in white feathers.

I no longer had any emotions. I was spent. I was void of any feelings at all. I had quit life.

With no real hope of any decent future, Vickie decided to take her life by her own hand. In her own words:

"I was high and drunk, I put a .357 in my mouth.

I was ready to pull the trigger when the glory of God dropped on my room in the bordello. The room completely filled with what I thought was gray smoke, but it smelled like lilacs. I attempted to pull the trigger, and a hand came between the trigger and the bullet. In the wrist of the hand was a hole and a voice said, "Now you belong to Me. You are Mine."

The man standing over me was Jesus.

I jumped up and started screaming at the top of my lungs as loud as I could:

"He is real! Jesus is real!"

All the girls that worked at Eadie's came running to my room and fell to the floor on their faces the minute they were at the door to my room. Little did I know then that He had delivered me from all my drug addictions, my alcoholism, my epilepsy, and dyslexia.

I got up, got dressed, walked down to my motor home with the Glory of God still on my body, leaving everything behind except the clothes on my back and my purse. I drove 25 miles to Sterling, Alaska.

The glory lifted from my body; I figured this must be where He wanted me to be. I parked at the Moose River campgrounds and stayed there.

No money, no food, no clothes, just the Master, myself, and Celeste, my sister."

Chapter Three

The Early Years

He also brought me up out of a horrible pit,
Out of the miry clay,
And set my feet upon a rock,
And established my steps.
He has put a new song in my mouth—
Praise to our God;
Many will see it and fear,
And will trust in the Lord.

Psalm 40:2-3

Vickie says, "I walked out of the bordello, so did Celeste, and we never looked back. That was over 40 years ago, and I have stood on my faith knowing that God has redeemed every sin in my life. No one can throw my past up in my face. It is my testimony. I have endured the hatred of my past by those who call themselves religious; yet, I am understood by the common man on the street, the ones who can relate, the ones who battle their own demons every day."

"My childhood has been redeemed with every child I have helped. My youth has been redeemed with every runaway who has found their self-worth. My drug habits and drunkenness have been redeemed with every person who is born again and Spirit-filled. God has used my life to start churches, schools, feeding programs, medical centers, and to create jobs globally."

"Jesus redeemed me," she says. "He paid the price for my life, and He used every heartbreak and degradation I experienced for His glory and for my good (Romans 8:28). He wanted me to be able to meet people right where they are, and they can look at my life and see there is hope for them."

"This I know, Jesus is real, God is my Father, and the Holy Spirit has guided me every single day since the day He met me in the bordello. All sins are redeemable. You don't have to wait for perfection," she explains.

"Redemption, so sweet the sound; but the cost, the price paid, is often untold. We didn't pay the price. Jesus did, the day He hung on the cross."

Jesus told Vickie, "Everything you know is wrong."

~~~

One thing is for certain, when God has work for us to do, He opens doors for us we can't even see, and one warm summer day, He did just that for Vickie. Remember that motion picture called *The Fifth Floor* Vickie starred in, chronicling her days when she was locked up? Well, there was a residual check for several thousand dollars from the movie's earnings waiting for her at the post office, ready to be cashed! Sifting through the envelopes in a wooden box on the post office's countertop, there it was. She went to the bank and cashed it.

Vickie and Celeste used the money to buy Bibles – every version they could find. Vickie says, "We didn't know which one was the right one, so, we bought them all."

Vickie was dyslexic before Jesus healed her of her alcohol and drug addictions, so when He healed her, He healed her dyslexia, too. Finally, not only could she read, God also had taught her *how* to read during the miracle.

The Holy Spirit led her to read Matthew, Mark, Luke, and John. She could not read enough about the Man who appeared to her, the Man who changed her life!

Vickie was struck by the verses in the Book of Mark 16:14-18:

"Later He appeared to the eleven as they sat at the table;
and He rebuked their unbelief and hardness of heart,
because they did not believe those who had seen Him after He had risen.
And He said to them,
"Go into all the world and preach the gospel to every creature.
He who believes and is baptized will be saved;
but he who does not believe will be condemned.
And these signs will follow those who believe:
In My name they will cast out demons;
they will speak with new tongues;
they will take up serpents;
and if they drink anything deadly, it will by no means hurt them;
they will lay hands on the sick, and they will recover."

As soon as she read Mark 16, even though she was a baby in Christ, she knew she could trust Jesus and believed every word she read. She spoke in new tongues like it said, she battled demons in His name, and she started praying for the sick. Vickie thought all Christians did this. The Bible said, "These signs will follow those who believe" (Mark 16:17), each according to God's will for those who are born again.

She understood miracles, signs, and wonders were for the believers. Vickie thought Christians had been doing this their entire lives. "It's written right here!" she proclaimed.

In her 30s already, she figured she had a lot of catching up to do, so she went out and followed Jesus' simple instructions, doing these things powered by His Holy Spirit. She believed that with Him she could do anything (Mark 9:23), just as He said.

So, she went out and did them in His name.

~~~

Vickie read God's Word and prayed constantly. She tells of how she was compelled to devour the Word of God. She was always asking God, "Who, what, where, and why," learning as much as she could, as fast as she could.

When she went to the different churches in the area, she was treated extremely badly because they only knew her by her worldly reputation as a prostitute and a stripper.

Nonetheless, God sent Vickie out to evangelize in the town and villages she came from, and whether people liked her or not, she didn't stop. Vickie and Celeste would gather with others in their home to study the Bible with great fervency and excitement.

Celeste studied the Bible in a theological way while Vickie preached His Word, both women led by His Holy Spirit. The gatherings grew to the point that they had to rent a room above a bar on the Kenai River on Sundays. They quickly grew out of that room and had to rent a building.

In the interim, Vickie put ads in the newspaper searching for a pastor.

Potential pastors would come out and meet Vickie, saying things like, "Your anointing is too strong, we can't compete." This seemed very strange to her.

Finally, a man named Paul came from another state. He took over the people who were gathering with Celeste and Vickie, a group in their small area which had grown in size to over 400 people. That was considered a good-sized church at the time. It was called the Foursquare Church.

On Resurrection Day, also known as Easter Sunday to some people, Vickie asked the Lord what to wear to church to bring honor to His name. She got all dressed up in a new outfit, went to the church, and stood in front of the big bay windows to pray, not realizing the men could see through her pretty maxi skirt. She could see the men and women snickering while she was speaking. She recognized several of the men in the congregation as former customers of hers at Eadie's.

Not one woman came up to Vickie to tell her the sunlight was going right through her clothing. Everyone could see everything under her dress as she was praying.

Of course, Vickie was extremely hurt and very, very angry when she found out. She went home after the service and asked God to forgive her; she read her Bible and prayed some more.

The next Sunday, when she went back to that same Foursquare Church, Vickie watched people walking in and out of the building, but when she grabbed the door handle, it was locked shut. No matter what she tried to do, the doors wouldn't open.

Vickie thought God was preventing her from going into the church because of the mistake she had made with her clothing the week before. She thought God didn't want her anymore. She watched the other people come and go, but they would slam the door shut when she tried to get in.

Vickie went to her car and began driving home.

She was crying so hard she had to pull to the side of the road. Sobbing and yelling at God in her "innocence and ignorance"

(Vickie's own words), she proclaimed as she shook her fist at Him, "Though You don't want me in the church you used me to build for You, I will see to it that a million people will get saved, and when You ask them who told them about You, they will tell You my name."

Vickie drove home, changed clothes, and went back to praying in the Spirit and reading her Bible.

~~~

A few years after being saved by Jesus, Vickie called her Mother, to make sure she was welcome to come and see her. God had brought her to an understanding of why her mother had endured the abuse from her husband, who was Vickie's father, for all of those years.

Her mother welcomed her with open arms. Vickie knew in her heart the lifestyle she had led was wrong and needed to ask her mother for forgiveness.

Vickie's mother, Olive, was a gentle woman of great beauty when she fell in love with Dutch, Vickie's father. Dutch's mother had raised him in a sturdy, good household. His mother was the grandma Vickie loved, the one with crayons and cookies, who took her to church when she was a toddler.

Sitting in a big, overstuffed chair in the living room, her mother listened to her with love beyond measure. Vickie was sitting on the floor at her feet when she poured out her heart, telling her mother everything. She put her head in her mother's lap and wept.

Vickie's mother forgave her immediately; they began a relationship that would last almost twenty years. Vickie finally got to know her mother's tender heart, her tough stamina, and the grace that carried her through all of those torturous years with her alcoholic husband.

She had stayed married to him all of those years for the sake of her children. After all, they were married in the 1940s, she was a Catholic, and wives simply did not divorce their husbands. Women at that time were counseled by the priests to, "Sleep in the beds they'd made for themselves and examine what was wrong with themselves to make their husbands behave the way they did."

Pain blurs memories. Olive lovingly filled in the blanks for Vickie; they both spent close to two decades sharing stories and healing together by the grace of God. In Vickie's own words, her mother was "an incredible woman."

~~~

Around the same time, remember the handsome man who looked cool in his white sweater at Eadie's bar? The man who just wanted to get to know Vickie, which was different than other men? The man Vickie warmed up to, who seemed to be a dependable person, secure in who he was, and didn't criticize or gossip about people? The man she could tell was a hard worker?

Well, his name was David, and they began to spend more and more time together. He managed a large oil company in Kenai, Alaska, not far from where Vickie had settled with Celeste.

Soon, they decided to move in together.

Every morning, Vickie continued to read and study her Bible. One day, she got to a part she did not understand. It was 1 Corinthians 6:9-10 and it said,

> *Do you not know that the unrighteous will not inherit*
> *the kingdom of God?*
> *Do not be deceived.*
> *Neither fornicators, nor idolaters, nor adulterers,*
> *nor homosexuals, nor sodomites, nor thieves, nor covetous,*
> *nor drunkards, nor revilers, nor extortioners*
> *will inherit the kingdom of God.*

She knew all of the words except one. She looked up the word "fornicators." There it was, it meant, "sexual intercourse between two persons not married to each other."

Vickie certainly was not going to take any chances with her newfound salvation and inheritance in the kingdom of God!

She packed up all of David's belongings and placed them on the front porch.

When David got home, he was confused. Vickie explained what she read and told him they could no longer fornicate, and that meant not living together. He replied, "Oh, that's alright, I'm Catholic." Vickie wasn't buying it and was not about to take any chances.

They were married the following week.

~~~

Vickie began traveling to revivals and conferences, eager to learn as much as she could for the glory of God. One day, she found herself at a revival where the preacher was talking about the gifts of the Holy Spirit as described in 1 Corinthians 12:4-11:

There are different kinds of gifts.
But it is the same Holy Spirit Who gives them.
There are different kinds of work to be done for Him.
But the work is for the same Lord.
There are different ways of doing His work.
But it is the same God who uses all these ways in all people.
The Holy Spirit works in each person in one way or another for the good of all.
One person is given the gift of teaching words of wisdom.
Another person is given the gift of teaching what he has learned and knows.
These gifts are by the same Holy Spirit.
One person receives the gift of faith.
Another person receives the gifts of healing.
These gifts are given by the same Holy Spirit.
One person is given the gift of doing powerful works.

Another person is given
the gift of speaking God's Word.
Another person is given the gift of telling the difference
between the Holy Spirit and false spirits.
Another person is given the gift of speaking in special sounds.
Another person is given the gift
of telling what these special sounds mean.
But it is the same Holy Spirit, the Spirit of God,
Who does all these things. He gives to each person as He wants to give.

Vickie stood up and raised her hand to get the preacher's attention. He clearly was annoyed by the interruption. He asked what she wanted. Vickie replied, "You are talking about these gifts of the Holy Spirit. I want them. How do I get them?"

He asked her to please sit down.

A few minutes later, same thing.

Finally, Vickie stood back up and asked the participants in the audience. "Who else wants these gifts?"

Twenty or so people stood up.

And right then and there, the Holy Spirit baptized and granted those people His precious gifts.

Vickie immediately understood, "But the righteous are bold as a lion" (Proverbs 28:1).

~~~

Jesus appeared to Vickie a second time around this time.

"Four years after Jesus appeared to me and saved my life in Eadie's brothel, He visited me again. He showed me my first heavenly vision – a tombstone with my husband's name on it and that date.

Jesus held my head against His chest. He was weeping over me.

I spoke to Him with my mind, 'Why are you weeping over me?' I thought I was doing something wrong.

His answer was, 'Because of all you are going to go through for Me.'"

God knew the wonderful man I had married was still drinking and was extremely prideful. A former Marine, he managed a large oil company in Kenai and was tough as nails. He had done some hellacious things against our marriage, and my heart was broken. I had threatened to divorce him. I remember very plainly God speaking to my mind at that moment, telling me if I divorced him, I had the right to, He would still be my Lord God.

The Lord told me to call my husband on the oil platform because he was standing on the very edge of it. I didn't want to make the call, but the Lord said, "If you don't fight for his soul, who will?"

So, I called him and stated, "I don't know if I love you, but I am still here."

At that moment, my sister Celeste came through the front door and fell flat on her face onto the cement floor screaming, "God's here! God's here!"

That night, when my husband came home, he gave his life to Christ. I baptized him in water and in the Holy Spirit.

Since that day, my husband David has been the backbone of everything I do. He built the church buildings and funded my work abroad. He is a holy example of how the greatest in God's kingdom serve...they do not wait to be served.

Today, at the age of seventy, he mentors people in the church.

He isn't a religious man; he is a Christian man.

Chapter Four

A Woman Who Serves

No weapon formed against you shall prosper,
And every tongue which rises against you in judgment
You shall condemn.
This is the heritage of the servants of the Lord,
And their righteousness is from Me,"
Says the Lord.

Isaiah 54:17

Vickie recalls:

When my sister and I were baptized in the Holy Spirit – born again – word traveled quickly. Everyone knew us as the former strippers and prostitutes Jesus saved. We were approached by the presbyters of churches in Alaska, Washington, Oregon, Idaho, California…they wanted us to travel to their churches to talk about what happened.

Mark 16:15-20 says, "…these signs will follow those who believe." When I read those verses in the Bible, I told Celeste we have work to do. "We are old, and we have to catch up." I told her we had to go to Anchorage and pray for the sick, the demonically oppressed. So off we went.

We arrived at the first big hospital and went from room to room praying over the patients. We watched as God healed all of them, just as He had healed us. God honored our faith, in our ignorance, as we went up from floor to floor. We thought all Christians did this.

People were miraculously healed and were walking out of the hospital. The doctors and nurses were taken aback, not understanding what was happening. Word spread quickly… other hospital workers heard what was happening and found us – the dishwashers, the janitors, they all came up to the place where we were. God was setting them free from any sickness and ailments, too.

Celeste and I got to the top floor where the psychiatric department was located. By this time, the security guards and psychiatrists were very upset and ordered us to leave the premises.

God had almost emptied the hospital through our faithfulness. People were being miraculously healed.

When hospital administrators ran us out of one place, we went to another. The word spread very quickly.

Another time, we traveled to the Alaska Psychiatric Institute. I knew an intern there named Larry. He was going to show us where the disturbed people slept. When we got there, the room was empty. He wondered where all the people had gone, so we went looking for them in another one of the big rooms. That room also appeared to be empty, but then we noticed a sheet pulled down to the floor. The patients were hiding under their beds under sheets.

Larry asked me what I was doing, I told him, "All I am doing is praying in tongues like in Acts 2:4 and 1 Corinthians 14:18." Apparently, the Holy Spirit's presence was so strong it agitated the demonic spirits within the patients causing them to go into hiding.

Word travels fast when people are miraculously healed in hospitals. The hospitals start losing money. We were no longer welcome at those places.

God opened whole towns and villages to us. That was even more miraculous to me.

When I preached in Sterling and Anchorage, Alaska, word spread fast about the crazy ex-stripper who was teaching the Word of God. People would tell their pastors, and one thing led to another. My days became filled with going from one church to another, preaching God's Word.

The Lord brought people into my life; I didn't want to leave my community, but He had other plans for me.

Later that year, I attended a conference in Oklahoma where I was introduced to well-known evangelists and preachers who were rooting themselves deeply into the false gospel of prosperity. There they were again – men wanting to use me, telling me to get all dolled-up in furs and jewelry to attract new members to their fake churches. They told me it was easy money... 90% show, 10% work, and 0% gospel. I got out of there in a hurry.

~~~

Vickie's trips were always paid for by her husband. David always stood beside her. Vickie lovingly recalls the biblical story of Priscilla and Aquila in describing the carrying out of their divine appointments.

Celeste, a shy woman, often stayed behind studying Scripture while Vickie's travels took her to faraway places during those first few years.

In 1985, Vickie traveled to the Philippines to speak at a conference. There, she witnessed miraculous healings, leading thousands to salvation. She almost died of cholera while there.

In her own words,

> I got cholera in Manila at Jacob's Well. It used to be a guest house in Manila. Because I was the only woman on the team that went to Manila that didn't have a chaperone, they put me in a different place.
>
> The place had a swimming pool, and I went swimming. That night I got deathly sick. Nobody had told me the pool was contaminated. It was not intentional...there was a language barrier...I don't speak Filipino.
>
> The international prayer team I went with had no regard for me whatsoever. I learned how, when a person moves dynamically in the anointing of God, you must know who you are and rely on God completely. People – it is the nature of the beast – will become jealous and envious of you, and you won't quite fit in with the group. I have never fit in, and I never will. Jesus didn't either.
>
> No one knew I was sick. No one came to check on me.
>
> Anyway, for five days and nights, I was on the shower floor with the cold water running on me, so sick I couldn't move; I

was vomiting and defecating right where I was. When I finally had enough strength to get up, it turned out it was the day I was supposed to speak.

I crawled to my bed from the shower and rolled on the bed itself to dry myself off. I had no energy and had lost a tremendous amount of weight. I was already thin before the cholera. I made it to the stadium where I was to be the opening speaker.

I prayed, "Lord, if you're gonna take me home, take me home in the pulpit." I bowed my head.

When I bowed my head, the power of God hit me, and I was knocked several feet backwards. I got up completely healed.

That service was powerfully anointing...the blind saw, the deaf heard, miraculous healings, all by the incredible dynamic power of God. Yet again, God honored my faithfulness to Him.

~~~

Vickie always told people, and continues to say to this day, "He saved me, and He will save you, too! Live each day as though it is your last one. Let go of you, let Him work through you!"

She often quotes:

For there is no respect of persons with God.
For as many as have sinned without law
shall also perish without law:
and as many as have sinned in the law shall be judged by the law;
(For not the hearers of the law are just before God,
but the doers of the law shall be justified.
For when the Gentiles, which have not the law,
do by nature the things contained in the law,

these, having not the law, are a law unto themselves:
Which shew the work of the law written in their hearts,
their conscience also bearing witness,
and their thoughts the mean while accusing or else excusing one
another;)
In the day when God shall judge the secrets of men
by Jesus Christ according to my gospel.
Romans 2:11-16

~~~

In 1984, Vickie and Celeste started the Ministry of the Living Stones in Sterling, Alaska, and in 1992, they started the second Ministry of the Living Stones in Anchorage, Alaska.

During those years, Vickie continued to travel, witnessing thousands of healings and hearts surrendered to Jesus Christ. The Lord used her to start hundreds of ministries worldwide, wherever God took her.

Coming to Him as to a living stone,
rejected indeed by men,
but chosen by God and precious,
you also, as living stones,
are being built up a spiritual house, a holy priesthood,
to offer up spiritual sacrifices
acceptable to God through Jesus Christ.
1 Peter 2:4-5

To this day, Vickie absolutely, joyfully insists we put the Lord God in front of everything... not just of ourselves, but in front of everything and everyone. She teaches how, when we do this, we will know true worship of our loving, Almighty God. She often says,

"Having a bad day? Sing loud! Sing so loud in worship to our Creator that you can't hear yourself think!"

"Do everything," she says, "in His love and the building of His Kingdom."

Vickie reminds us it was the religious who killed Christ, the religious system of His day. The ministries she has been blessed to start are not "religious."

"It is not a religious system; it is a way of life. We must push past our flesh into the Spirit realm to serve the Almighty with the labor of our hands," she says.

She reminds us: "The hands of the righteous are blessed (Psalm 90:17); if you are faithful with a little, you will be trusted with much (Luke 16:10); and, out of the abundance of your heart, much is given (Luke 8:15).

"Seek the fruit of the Spirit, not the fruit of the flesh," she cautions. "God is the Author and the Finisher of our faith."

"Allow the Lord of your life, BE the Lord of your Life!" she proclaims.

~~~

"I have been blessed to be used as a valued vessel of God since the day I walked out of that whorehouse," Vickie says, "Religion will not save you, only GOD can save you!"

~~~

In 1984, Vickie built and opened the Academy of Higher Learning for K-12 in Sterling, Alaska. God's hand being on everything she does, it was accredited by the State and drew excellent teachers, including one who was a recipient of the Christa McAuliffe Award for Excellence in Teacher Education.

Children at the Academy were taught the basic skills to successfully navigate secular life; more importantly, they were infused with God's Word, ensuring their successful navigation toward eternity in heaven with their Creator.

"People need to learn they cannot rely on their own understanding of His Word; we must depend completely on the Holy Spirit to give us wisdom and insight." Vickie teaches how having only limited knowledge coupled with limited, earthly understanding is a dangerous weapon used in tyranny. She shows us how organized religion does just that.

Recall how Jesus told her, "Everything you know is wrong," when he saved her that day in the brothel. She knows now the Truth in His words...without His love as the foundation of everything we do, we will not accomplish anything worthwhile for the building of His kingdom.

Jesus told us,

And I will pray the Father, and He will give you another Helper,
that He may abide with you forever –
the Spirit of truth, whom the world cannot receive,
because it neither sees Him nor knows Him;
but you know Him, for He dwells with you and will be in you.
I will not leave you orphans; I will come to you.
"A little while longer and the world will see Me no more,
but you will see Me.
Because I live, you will live also.
At that day you will know that I am in My Father, and you in Me,
and I in you.
He who has My commandments and keeps them,
it is he who loves Me.
And he who loves Me will be loved by My Father,
and I will love him and manifest Myself to him."
John 14:16-21

"You have to live by faith. It's that simple. Kill all the snakes of religion. Paul was not in the upper room, yet God filled him with the Holy Spirit. Religion will tell you the Holy Spirit only comes through the 12 apostles. That's not true. That's a lie. You do not get to God through apostolic succession. You get to God through faith." (Hebrews 11:1).

Vickie challenges us all, "Do you have the faith of the four?" She's talking about the faith of the four men who lowered the sick man to Jesus through the rooftop for healing in Luke 5:17-39.

Vickie explains that on the Day of Pentecost, out of the 500 people who initially gathered in the upper room, only 120 men and women were left waiting, anticipating the appearance of the Lord's Holy Spirit, just as Jesus had foretold. Those 120 souls received the Holy Spirit along with His gifts. Women were in that room, too, and they were filled with His Holy Spirit. And she goes on to say that the descendants of the other 380 – the ones who left before the Holy Spirit arrived – are still walking around today telling people miracles stopped when Jesus left the earth. They weren't there. They don't know and will not listen. They are not teachable; they do not know. They lie. They left the upper room. They did not receive the power of the Holy Spirit. "They just don't know," she says.

"There is nothing about apostolic succession or the merit of man-made traditions in God's Word – not one word! Anyone who thinks they're all that important, who lie about this, are dead wrong. God calls whom He calls to serve – in His love and His Truth – and no one has the right to say otherwise," Vickie says emphatically. Grateful to be filled with the Holy Spirit, she knows this firsthand.

"He saved me from myself that day in the bordello, and He will save you, too, if you let Him," she often says.

In 1997, the Lord used Vickie to establish the Ministry of the Living Stones Bible Institute of Alaska.

~~~

Servanthood is a way of living for those who love and follow Jesus (Matthew 22:14). Mark 10:45 tells us, "For even the Son of Man did not come to be served, but to serve, and to give His life a ransom for many."

Vickie stresses, in her love for God and for each one of us whom she teaches, that we should live a life of service, putting God ahead of any and all other considerations. She teaches, "God first, our spouses and our family in Jesus Christ, second, and then everything else follows," as the order for anyone who is striving to live a holy life.

Vickie sees herself as a humbled, forgiven handmaiden of the Lord. This is how she wants to be remembered – as an example of the way in which we should all aim to live, serving the Lord God, devoted to Him in every circumstance of our lives. Her life as a chosen handmaid is obvious in her obedience and complete faith in Him.

But those who wait on the Lord
Shall renew their strength;
They shall mount up with wings like eagles,
They shall run and not be weary,
They shall walk and not faint.
Isaiah 40:31

Chapter Five

Blessed

Then He lifted up His eyes toward His disciples, and said:

"Blessed are you poor,
For yours is the kingdom of God.
Blessed are you who hunger now,
For you shall be filled.
Blessed are you who weep now,
For you shall laugh.
Blessed are you when men hate you,
And when they exclude you,
And revile you, and cast out your name as evil,
For the Son of Man's sake.
Rejoice in that day and leap for joy!
For indeed your reward is great in heaven,
For in like manner their fathers did to the prophets."

Luke 6:20-23

Together with others before her who were called to carry the mantle of the Lord, Vickie also became a living, walking, teaching epistle, and remains so today. Gifted by God to see in the supernatural, she depends on the Lord God for everything and knows through Him she can do anything (Philippians 4:13).

This anointing is the Power of God, given to meet the needs of hurting humanity, through His Holy Spirit.

Vickie often says, "I am a willing vessel God uses. He lifted me up out of the bordello, and He will use you, too." She adds, "It feels extremely humbling that God the Father and His precious Holy Spirit would entrust someone like me to do His will and work."

"The Power of His Holy Spirit was sent to us to help us," she says. "God chooses His servants, knowing each one of us when we were being knit together in our mother's wombs." (Psalm 139:13)

When a person invites God's Holy Spirit into their life, the miraculous takes place. This holy anointing is known in the Spirit. This is not an earthly phenomenon, rather, it is supernatural. It is a person coming into contact with the living God – the Creator of heaven and earth, whose Spirit is with us. This power – this anointing – was promised to us by Jesus (Acts 1:8).

Vickie was separated from everything she knew the day Jesus appeared to her in the brothel. She became His loyal handmaiden that day; He gave her the gift of His precious Holy Spirit.

Indeed, when we become willing vessels for Him, He separates us.

Why was David in the field alone as a shepherd, away from his family? God did not want him to be contaminated. God separates those He calls from the world they knew. Same with Job. Same with Vickie.

Vickie often says, "Praise Him in your separation! If God is pleased, what more do you want?" He has a divine purpose for your life.

Jesus said, "'I am the way, the Truth and the Life. No one comes to the Father except through Me'" (John 14:6).

~~~

Why Jesus? Vickie shines light on the subject, "Look at all the other religions. Their founders are dead. Muhammad, Buddha, Charles Taze Russell (Jehovah's Witnesses), Joseph Smith (Mormons/Latter Day Saints), Confucius. The list goes on. Not one of them came alive again after their death. Jesus rose from death, promising eternal life to each one of us. Jesus is alive, is with us, through the power of the Holy Spirit. Jesus promised, 'I will send you a Comforter' (John 14), He said, 'You will rise again' (1 John 2:25). No one else can claim that.

I asked Vickie to describe the Holy Spirit. She responded, "He is incomparable. He is the third Person in the Trinity, and we must give Him the respect that is due Him, the same as the Father who 'thinks,' and the Son who 'speaks' – His Holy Spirit 'creates.' (Genesis 1:2)"

Mind, Body and Spirit – the Trinity is one Person, His Holy Spirit is the Person who is with us. She continues, "The Holy Spirit is my friend, my confidante. He is phenomenal. I don't deserve Him, but He stays with me anyway. He's a gentleman, He does not force me to do anything. He saved my life – not once, but twice."

The second time He saved me from certain death was when I was snowmobiling in Alaska during a blizzard with white-out conditions. I heard His voice audibly say, "Stop!" I was headed for a 300-foot cliff without realizing it! I stopped. I know the Holy Spirit saved my life.

~~~

Since God can do whatever He wants to do, whenever He wants to do it, a person can receive God's anointing in several ways. It can be taken away as quickly as it is given, too. A great example is this, found in the Book of Acts, which reads, "God did extraordinary miracles through Paul, so that even handkerchiefs and aprons that had touched him were taken to the sick, and their illnesses were cured and the evil spirits left them" (Acts 19:11-12).

The apostles and the men and women in the upper room, who received the Holy Spirit on the Day of Pentecost, did not rush around laying hands on people to impart an experience of fire or power after they received the gifts (John 15:16-27). They did not chant words, nor did they expect healings and miracles, or other supernatural events following their Baptism in the Holy Spirit. They just KNEW God would work through each one of them for His Glory and their good (Romans 8:28) according to His will for them.

The Holy Spirit does exactly that for us – He comforts us, helps us, moves within our hearts to guide us, direct us, and help us when we open our hearts to Him.

The account of the woman touching the hem of the Lord's garment is a wonderful example of how He is here for us in our faith and love for Him. Hers is a story of immense faith; she had determined in her own mind that if she could only touch His clothing she would be healed. When Jesus felt her touch, He turned to her and said, *"Take heart, daughter, your faith has healed you"* (Matthew 9:22).

It wasn't that His cloak held any power, it wasn't anything magical like Simon the Sorcerer thought it to be; rather, her faith was such that she believed that even touching what Jesus was wearing would heal her.

And, He did.

~~~

Vickie teaches, "He intercedes for us as our Comforter in times of need and our Counselor when we need direction," (John 14:26-28), and our Advocate when no one else is there for us (1 John 2:1). "Believe Him when He tells you He loves you!" she says. "Have the faith of a child, for faith is the assurance of things hoped for, the conviction of things not seen" (Hebrews 11:1).

Do you not know that you are a temple of God
and that the Spirit of God dwells in you?
If anyone destroys the temple of God,
God will destroy that person;
for the temple of God is holy, and that is what you are.
1 Corinthians 3:16-17

Asked to describe what "anointing" is, Vickie explained this way: "Anointing is the presence of God, the power of the Holy Spirit that overshadows you, leads you, fills your mouth according to the Scripture you are preaching; without the presence of God, it is a dead service. It is the anointing, the Holy Spirit of God, that moves across the congregation, no matter how small or large, that transfers the Word from the speaker to the hearer. It is what makes the deaf hear and the lame walk. The anointing is a must for any ministry to be founded and to grow. The gift and call is without repentance, but the anointing must be tended to by seeking the Lord with fasting, prayer, and reading the bible. Without the anointing it is a soul work, it is a flesh work, it is a repetitive work; the Spirit of God keeps things fresh, and it always seems new to the hearer. The anointing is ever changing as we grow and mature in Him."

The Gifts of the Holy Spirit work freely through Vickie. They are: Knowledge, Wisdom, Healings, Faith, Miracles, Prophesy, Distinguishing of Spirits, and Tongues/Interpretation of Tongues; God blesses her to operate in all of them for His glory and for the good of His people, to bring more souls into His kingdom.

Asked about this gifting, Vickie says, "If you were the only person on an island, that was a believing Christian, how many of these wonderful gifts would God have you move in? You would evangelize, prophesy, heal the sick, receive Words of Wisdom, Words of Knowledge. It is very, very simple. When you trust in Christ, and if you are willing to be moved by the Spirit of God, He will use you. If you aren't prideful, God will use you in all these gifts. They are all from Him and are available to those who love Him who are willing to serve Him."

~ ~ ~

Jesus appeared to Vickie two times – she is blessed to walk in the powerful anointing of the Holy Spirit. Yet, there are men who tell her she is to sit down and be quiet, scolding her that women are not to teach or preach.

Vickie answers them with a few choice words, always delivered with the love of God's Truth, telling them they are misinformed and that they are overcome by the demonic spirit of religion. She encourages them to read the Bible because there are literally dozens of passages to the contrary. She often cites this passage to them from His Word:

"Therefore, if you died with Christ from the basic principles of the world,

why, as though living in the world, do you subject yourselves to regulations—

"Do not touch, do not taste, do not handle,"

which all concern things which perish with the using—

according to the commandments and doctrines of men?

These things indeed have an appearance of wisdom in self-imposed religion,

false humility, and neglect of the body,

but are of no value against the indulgence of the flesh."

Colossians 2:20-23

Many remain not only unconvinced, but become hostile, quoting this, "Let your women keep silent in the churches, for they are not permitted to speak; but they are to be submissive, as the law also says" (1 Corinthians 14:34).

God will always bring people into our lives who will help us better understand His Word, and in 1985 He brought Charles Trombley and Vickie together at a conference where they were both speaking. Trombley is the author of *Who Said Women Can't Teach?* It's an excellent book that Vickie often recommends.

"God chooses whom He chooses," she says, "Women will not be silenced; the enemy will be silenced."

There were women elders in the Bible. Several women are mentioned as leaders and prophets of Israel, including Miriam (Exodus 15:20), Deborah (Judges 4:4-5), Esther (Esther 4:15-17), Huldah (2 Kings 22:14). Women held important positions in the early church (Acts 1:12-14, Acts 18:24-26, Acts 21:7-9, and Romans 16:1-16).

Much of the opposition to women in ministry is based on two passages: 1 Corinthians 14: 33-35 and 1Timothy 2:11-12. As with all of the Bible, some background information is necessary for understanding these passages.

Vickie will tell you, "It is important to remember that the apostle Paul proclaimed that all believers are equal in God's sight,"

For you are all sons of God through faith in Christ Jesus.
For as many of you as were baptized into Christ have put on Christ.
There is neither Jew nor Greek,
there is neither slave nor free,
there is neither male nor female;
for you are all one in Christ Jesus.
And if you are Christ's,
then you are Abraham's seed,
and heirs according to the promise.
Galatians 3:26-29

Vickie encourages everyone to read Romans 16 regarding this topic. Paul describes a deacon as an overseer. Nowhere does it say women cannot be leaders, pastors. Paul says women can prophesy.

He greets "Priscilla and Aquila," the husband-and-wife team, placing Priscilla first because he knows she is the leader, never diminishing the role of her beloved husband, Aquila, as her protector and benefactor.

"The Word of God is not to be manipulated. Man's traditions and personal experiences have no place in Scripture," Vickie says, "The outpouring of the Holy Spirit was on both men and women."

The only reason Jesus chose twelve men to be His apostles is because women would not have been accepted per the existing Jewish law at that time. Jesus knew this. After Jesus fulfilled the law of the Old Testament by His death and resurrection, He opened the door to everyone, to all who are one in our Christ Jesus – both men and women.

If God has raised a woman up to lead, to serve, how dare we, as humans, condemn the person God has chosen.

"Let the Holy Spirit call and anoint. Let God be God!" Vickie extols.

There are many excellent books written about women teaching and preaching. Trombley's book explains these precepts clearly and scholarly.

Vickie and Trombley both came "out of the garbage of the 90s" (her words), meeting each other when they were ministering at the same place in Seattle in the 90s. The "garbage of the 90s" was littered with scripture taken out of context, allowing false gospels to prevail.

Here's an excellent excerpt from Trombley's book to the men who insist women need to be silent in church, those who think women should never preach or teach:

> When a male Jew repented of his sins and crowned Jesus as both Lord and Christ, he became a new creature, and a participant in the New Covenant. However, most of them stayed within the framework of Judaism, keeping both the law and customs. It was these Judaizers who insisted that the male gentiles must be circumcised and keep the customs of Moses.

And these same Judaizers went after the Christian women. "Let the women keep silent in the churches; for they are not permitted to speak but let them subject themselves just as the Law also says" (1 Corinthians 14:34).

The oral Law wasn't inspired as was what is the Word of God, any more than *Matthew Henry's Commentary* or the *Pulpit Commentary* is inspired. The oral Law was made up of what the rabbis thought the Torah meant. They thought it said women were sexually seductive, mentally inferior, socially embarrassing, and spiritually separated from the law of Moses; therefore, let them be silent. It was the Jewish oral law, not the Bible, that demanded the silence of women. That law wasn't the original, inspired Word of God spoken through the mouth of holy men of God; it was Jewish traditionalism.

Sir William Ramsey, a former professor at the University of Aberdeen in Glasgow, was widely known for his thorough research into the history of Christianity in Asia Minor. He said, "We should be ready to suspect Paul is making a quotation from the letter addressed to him by the Corinthians whenever he alludes to their knowledge, or when any statement stands in marked contrast either with the immediate context or with Paul's known views."

Notice the controversial verses we're studying stand in marked contrast with verses 30-39 as well as with Paul's views expressed in 1 Corinthians 11:5. He said, "All may prophesy that all may learn," without any qualification as to whether men or women were prophesying. Then he abruptly, and totally out of context, dropped his teaching on the spiritual gifts and tackled the question of women being silent. Because it is in such marked contrast, some commentators have deliberately rearranged the order of these verses and place them after verses 39-40 so Paul's theme would be uninterrupted. However, these verses are exactly where the Holy Spirit inspired Paul to place them since they are directly related to the overall problem. The marked contrast separated them from Paul's views and teaching.

The Apostle Paul didn't say, "don't permit," but "it is not permitted,' suggesting someone else was doing the forbidding. The "it" would be the law since it is the law that says women must remain silent. No where does the Bible say it is a shame for women to speak; therefore, the "law" can't be the Bible. The other law, the oral law of the Jews, specifically directed women to remain silent.[5]

~~~

We can be certain Jesus did not appear to Vickie Walber expecting her to stay quiet. He did not bless her with the gifts of His Holy Spirit to silence her. He did not bless her with His grace and mercy so she could keep His Glory and His message of salvation to herself.

Trombley reminds us of this:

What can we say about Jesus's attitude toward women? It was positive, liberating and accepting. He defended them when they transgressed Jewish law if it was based on uninspired rabbinical interpretations. He didn't hesitate to withstand the social traditions and prejudices in order to free them. He accepted women as capable and fully equal with men in all things.

He closed the door to the Old Covenant and ushered in a New Covenant wherein there is neither Jew nor Greek, male nor female, only oneness in Christ. He set the captives free, both men and women, from all the bandages of sin, the curse, and religion.

Did Jesus say women can't teach? Does the Bible? Who did? The Judaizers relying on the oral law of the Jews.

Should women remain bound because of Christian traditions that are only human interpretations? No more than the women serving under Christ's ministry remained bound to the Jewish traditions.

My conclusion is this: Nowhere does the Bible from Genesis to maps prove forbid any woman from serving God in any capacity He calls and prepares her to fulfill.[6]

~ ~ ~

Remember, in the early days of Vickie's journey with the Lord God Almighty, she was crying so hard she had to pull to the side of the road after being supernaturally locked out of a church. Sobbing and yelling at God in her "innocence and ignorance" (Vickie's own words), she proclaimed as she shook her fist at Him, "Though You don't want me in the church you used me to build for You, I will see to it that a million people will get saved, and when You ask them who told them about You, they will tell You my name."

Would God intentionally silence half of His creation, who love Him and glorify Him?

Would He lift Vickie from the bordello that day and tell her to be quiet?

Of course not.

After forty-five years of preaching, teaching, and still going strong, there is a huge probability God has used her to reach over a million people already.

What then shall we say to these things?
If God is for us,
who can be against us?
Romans 8:31

Chapter Six

Firsthand

I will praise the Lord as long as I live.
I will sing praises to my God with my dying breath.

Psalm 146:2

God knows the outcome even when we can't see it. Having faith that God is with us means trusting Him in every situation, continuing to pray, and maintaining hope even when the situation seems impossible or hopeless. God brought Vickie into my life during one of those times.

~~~

When the going gets rough, we are strengthened by the promise in Romans 8:28, "And we know that God causes all things to work together for good to those who love God, to those who are called according to His purpose."

This life-changing moment comes to mind:

Midafternoon sunlight streaming through the stain-glass windows, I was practically alone in the little perpetual adoration chapel. There were a handful of ancient sisters sitting quietly in the surrounding pews. It was quiet and peaceful, and I began my silent prayer. *Dear Jesus Lord, keep my children safe, unbreak their hearts, heal them, heal me ... please ... please ...*

I nodded off, at least I thought I did. When I opened my eyes, I was sitting at a table at an outdoor cafe, a huge umbrella covering the whole table shielding it from the hot summer sun. I looked up and saw I was having lunch with Jesus. I sat up straight, looking down to make sure I was decently buttoned up.

A beggar approached our table. He was unkempt and dirty, bones protruding through his very soiled tattered garment. I reached to give him some food from my plate.

Jesus commanded, "No, don't do that!"

Startled, I looked up and said to Jesus, "but he's hungry! Didn't You tell us to feed the hungry, give drink to the thirsty, clothe the naked, visit the imprisoned?" ... I rattled off the corporal works of mercy straight from the Book of Matthew describing His own words from His Sermon on the Mount.

Then, I realized I was arguing with our Lord and Master Jesus Himself! I was embarrassed and stopped talking. I felt my face blush.

Jesus said softly, "Do not give him anything."

Totally confused, I asked Him, "I don't understand. Why not?"

Jesus said, "Because that's Satan. If you give him even the smallest piece of

anything, he will keep coming back for more and more until there is nothing left *of* you."

I was trying to do the right thing, the holy thing, following His holy directions, and I realized I had it all wrong! Thoughts swirled. I was caught off-guard, out of context, in a different dimension. I looked up at Him and asked, "How do I know when to give and who to give it to?"

"Trust Me," was His answer.

Immediately, I was delivered wide awake back to the wooden pew. I searched the chapel and thought loudly: *Wait! Wait! Don't go! Where are you?*

I realized, at that moment, I had no idea how to trust Him. I had no idea what it meant to trust Him. During my life, I had prayed, I had performed the works of mercy, I had taught my children how to pray, I had gone to church religiously, and yet, here I was, completely baffled.[7]

I realized at that moment, even though I thought I had trusted Him, I truly wasn't trusting Him at all, and I had no idea what this really meant or how to do it! Oh, I had been kidding myself, the reality was clear: I had no idea. I looked around, searched for Him, silently in my heart pleading for Him to return to tell me how to trust Him! I needed to know!

My "lunch" with Him that day changed my outlook. I realize now I was not alone during the long years I spent searching for Him to give me an answer. He was answering me with every breath I took, with every step I was taking moving toward Him. I truly think everyone goes through a time like I did, wanting to know if He's real, searching for answers. It's that ubiquitous "why" reverberating in our souls, our spirits, the universe, begging an answer.

I've come to know the "spiritual desert" is not a land of punishment. Truly, it's a place of discovery, refreshment, and refinement of the soul.

~ ~ ~

A few years later, I married a handsome, hard-working man named David. We moved to Alaska to begin our new life together. Long story shortened: we endured great hardship there for six long years. Alaska is a rough place. It's beautiful, but dangerous.

We all come to know, sooner or later, there's always a lesson to be learned no matter what the circumstance. I was grateful for the precious gift of hope; God's grace kept me going. I knew our loving and powerful Lord God was with us in our darkest of times. I had learned over the years to trust Him (Isaiah 25:1).

During this Alaskan nightmare, I had heard about a woman named Vickie who lived about an hour away from us. We had met many people who knew her personally. I believed she was a woman of faith, a woman who belonged to God, despite our Orthodox priest telling us she was not and to stay away from her.

You see, we had settled into an Antiochian Orthodox lifestyle. We left that church when we discovered the priest had misappropriated funds. Subsequently, we joined the Russian Orthodox Church.

Again, I was heartbroken when I was banned by the priest from receiving the sacraments after my husband and I refused to allow him and his family access to free services in the community. He was taking gross advantage of us. He expected David and me to foot the bills for a myriad of services because he was "a man of God, a man of the cloth." He felt my husband was generous and I was the mean one because I put a stop to his scheming.

After those two experiences, I began rethinking what I had heard about Vickie. Gossip kills, and clearly she had been gossiped about.

~~~

Jesus said, "For the Son of man did not come to destroy men's lives, but to save them. And they went to another village" (Luke 9:55-56).

We left Alaska and went back home.

~~~

The priest, his family, and others who had lied and gossiped about us too, caused serious legal problems for us. We needed help.

"And the power of the Lord was present to heal..." (Luke 5:17).

I knew Jesus redeemed and restored, performed healings and miracles, and saved a profoundly stricken humanity who had been deeply in need of His love and His mercy. God had rescued me from myself years before, and I knew He was with me.

David and I prayed like never before.

Because He is God, the Son of Man, in search of sinners, the Good Shepherd constantly looks for the sheep on the edge of the cliff, those who are broken and hurting, those who finally see Him and cry, "Help!"

And we were on that cliff.

Back home in Wisconsin, we needed a good attorney who was in Alaska, but trusting no one we had known there for a referral. In prayer, I remembered this woman named Vickie who truly was loved by the people who told us about her.

Call her, God whispered to my heart in prayer.

So, I did.

I had learned – the hard way, of course – to be obedient to His commands. I had come to know God always removed my heavy burdens and healed my heartaches. I had learned to trust Him, and now, He would be sending me one of His most magnificent teachers.

Little did I know, at the time, that my life would be changed forever.

~~~

I worked up the courage to contact this woman I had never met. I called Vickie.

~~~

We were on the phone for hours!

Amazing grace poured in, replacing any old cracks of stale gossip with the glory of God.

It became obvious why the priests gossiped about her being a cult leader. She was a threat to their money-making machines, a danger to their religious spirit of arrogance and self-righteousness, to which they were blind because of their own self-importance. The spirit of deception pushed heavily on their souls; gossip was a salve on their own sin.

Hours passed, Vickie and I continued talking to each other; it was as though time had stopped. There is no time in eternity (2 Peter 3:8), I could tell I was in a different place.

The room I was sitting in during our conversation filled with the most beautiful fragrance I had ever breathed in; it was the perfume of wildflowers and rain. It lingered for hours, long enough for my husband to ask about the lovely perfume I was wearing when he came home from work.

I didn't know how to answer; I learned later it was the beautiful fragrance of the presence of the Holy Spirit (2 Corinthians 2:15-17, Proverbs 27:9).

Vickie asked for nothing. She poured God's grace into my willing vessel freely, just as Christ Himself had done for her.

She told me during that conversation:

Religions have no power,

Jesus is handing the keys to the kingdom directly to us,

There is a Baptism in the Holy Spirit,

Miracles still happen,

The fruits of faith flourish in a heart filled with humility and gratitude,

Jesus is the same today as yesterday and tomorrow,

The Holy Spirit is with us,

Always give all glory to God for everything.

Oh, that's not all. That was only the beginning of the many lessons she would share with me.

Vickie has poured the love and the Word of God into anyone who was willing to listen. I don't remember how our conversation ended that day. Come to think of it, that conversation is still continuing to this day, twelve years later.

After a few months had passed, four thousand miles were traveled from Alaska to Wisconsin; we finally met each other in person in the lobby of P. F. Chang's at the local mall. Vickie had invited my husband and me to have dinner with her and her husband's family there. Her husband is from Wisconsin, and so is mine. Her husband's name is David, and so is mine. Her husband is an avid hunter, so is mine. They both are shorter than we are, and we are older than both of them. There are no coincidences in God's care. Our meeting was jaw-dropping for me on every level possible.

What are the chances the waitress and Vickie would know each other after meeting in the Philippines a few years earlier? Well, there they were, gabbing away like long-lost friends. The waitress asked Vickie to pray with her. They prayed together – there was an indescribable, uncontainable joy shared between them.

A few months later, Vickie returned to Wisconsin, and we were blessed with her staying at our house.

I must mention here, I was physically injured when I lived in Alaska – my spine was visibly curved to one side. The radiograph indicated my spine not only was curved to the left, it also was rotated. The doctors told me there was nothing they could do, there was no surgery to correct the extensive damage. They offered narcotic drugs to me to alleviate the pain. I declined.

My back frequently spasmed, a scoliotic hump had formed on the upper left side, my right leg was shorter than my left leg.

Vickie told me she felt sorry for me "limping around looking like Quasimodo." Those were her exact words describing what I looked like to her in my broken condition. Vickie has a marvelous sense of humor; her honest comment made me laugh.

She asked me if I believed Jesus could heal me.

Of course, I said yes, because I did and do believe this.

She asked if she could lay her hands on my back and pray. Of course, my answer was, "Yes."

Vickie included the imagery of the sky and the ocean in the prayer she prayed while laying her hands on my twisted back asking God to heal me. "If the sky was the parchment and the ocean was the inkwell, there would not be enough of either to write thank you letters to you forever for everything You do for us" (paraphrased from a hymn, *The Love of God*, written by Frederick Lehman in 1917). She continued to pray, "Jesus, please touch my sister through the power of the Holy Spirit, so that she will not end up looking like Quasimodo. I am asking in the name of You, Lord, to heal her now."

When Vickie finished praying in the Holy Spirit, she looked at me and told me to raise my arms above my head.

I did.

My back cracked and popped right up into the right side of my head! It continued to pop and crack for the rest of the day.

Thank you, Jesus! My back is straight! The hump is gone! My legs are the same length! I am healed! Thank you, Lord Jesus. Thank you. Psalm 146:2 says,

I will praise the Lord as long as I live.
I will sing praises to my God with my dying breath.

Yes, with faith the size of a mustard seed, because I had convinced myself I had used up any smidgeon of miracle-grace I had left, the Holy Spirit nonetheless saw that speck of belief in my heart and healed me, working through Vickie here on earth.

Vickie reminded me His love and mercy is endless for His children.

With deep gratitude and humility, these verses, in my heart, came to mind:

"'If you can?' Jesus said to him, 'Everything is possible for one who believes'" (Mark 9:23), "'But as for me, I would seek God, And I would place my cause before God, Who does great and unsearchable things, Wonders without number' (Job 5:8-9)."

And now, Lord, take note of their threats,
and grant that Your bondservants
may speak Your word with all confidence,
while You extend Your hand to heal,
and signs and wonders take place
through the name of Your holy servant Jesus.
And when they had prayed,
the place where they had gathered together was shaken,
and they were all filled with the Holy Spirit

and began to speak the word of God with boldness.
Acts 4:29-31

God had sent Vickie to me to show me how to open that door to our living Lord. I am forever grateful to her and to GOD for sending her to me. Vickie is my teacher, my mentor, my pastor – and has become my cherished, beloved sister in our Christ Jesus.

But Ruth said [to Naomi]:
"Entreat me not to leave you,
Or to turn back from following after you;
For wherever you go, I will go;
And wherever you lodge, I will lodge;
Your people shall be my people,
And your God, my God.
Ruth 1:16

Chapter Seven

An Interview With Vickie

Therefore, laying aside all malice, all deceit, hypocrisy, envy, and all evil speaking,
as newborn babes, desire the pure milk of the word,
that you may grow thereby, if indeed you have tasted that the Lord is gracious.

Coming to Him as to a living stone, rejected indeed by men,
but chosen by God and precious,

you also, as living stones, are being built up a spiritual house, a holy priesthood,
to offer up spiritual sacrifices acceptable to God through Jesus Christ.

Therefore, it is also contained in the Scripture,

"Behold, I lay in Zion
A chief cornerstone, elect, precious,
And he who believes on Him will by no means be put to shame."

Therefore, to you who believe, He is precious; but to those who are disobedient,

"The stone which the builders rejected
Has become the chief cornerstone,"

1 Peter 2:1-7

Did you have any inkling when you were a child of what God had planned for your life?

No, I didn't even know there was a loving God. I thought God was a dirty word, my mom and dad didn't go to church. My grandmother was Methodist, but they wouldn't let her sing, so she joined the Seventh Day Adventists, and they wouldn't let her sing, either. She is the person who taught me the little prayer "Now I lay me down to sleep..." and told me about how her father was part of a revival. I was only four or five years old and didn't know what the word "revival" meant. I remembered the word later in life, though. That was the extent of my knowledge of God.

When you went to the tent revival, what were you addicted to? Please describe what you experienced when your addictions were miraculously removed from you.

I was addicted to cocaine, heroin, opium, and was an alcoholic. When I went to the revival, I dressed ready for work because I didn't know what a revival was. None of my addictions were permanently removed at the revival. I would stand up every night and say the Sinner's Prayer, and then return for work at Eadie's bordello. No one told me to read a Bible.

Later, when Jesus appeared to you in the brothel, will you please describe what happened?

I was high and drunk, screaming at this person called Jesus, God. I used every foul word you could think of and told Him all He wanted was people's money, all He wanted was people's money. I did my hair and makeup. I dressed myself in a white peignoir flowing with ostrich feathers. I laid my head down on two pillows because I didn't want my sister to find my brains splattered on the walls. I put a .357 gun in my mouth and was ready to pull the trigger. The room completely filled with what I thought was smoke, but it smelled like lilacs. I attempted to pull the trigger, and a hand came between the trigger and the bullet. In the wrist of the hand was a hole, and a voice said, "Now you belong to Me, you are Mine." The man standing over me was Jesus. I jumped up and started screaming at the top of my lungs as loud as I could, "Jesus is real! Jesus is real!" All the girls that worked at Eadie's came running into my room and fell to the floor on their faces the minute they hit my door. Little did I know then that He had delivered me from all my drug addictions, my alcoholism, my epilepsy, and dyslexia. I got up, got dressed, walked down to my motor home with the glory of God still on my body. I left everything behind except the clothes on my back. I took my purse and drove 25 miles to Sterling, Alaska. The glory lifted from my body, and I figured this must be where He wants me. I parked at the Moose River campgrounds and stayed there. No money, no food, no clothes. Just the Master, myself, and Celeste, my sister.

The second time Jesus visited you, what happened? What was His message? How many years after His first appearance to you did he return to you?

It was four years after His first visitation. I had gotten married to a wonderful man who still drank, was extremely prideful, and managed a large oil company in Kenai. He had done some hellacious things; I threatened to divorce him. I remember very plainly God speaking to my mind and telling me if I divorce him, I had the right to, He would still be my Lord. He showed me my first vision of a tombstone with my husband's name on it and that date. He held my head against His chest after He had come down through my ceiling. He was weeping over me. I spoke to Him with my mind, "Why are you weeping over me?" His answer was, "Because of all you are going to go through for me." At that moment my sister came through the front door and fell flat on her face onto the cement floor screaming, "God's here! God's here!" The Lord told me to call my husband on the oil platform because he was standing on the very edge of it. I didn't want to make the call, but the Lord said, "If you don't fight for his soul, who will?" So, I called and stated, "I don't know if I love you, but I am still here." That night, when my husband came home, he gave his life to Christ. I baptized him in water and in the Holy Spirit.

80

You walk in the Holy Spirit Power of our Almighty God. What does that feel like to you?

It feels extremely humbling that God the Father and His precious Holy Spirit would entrust someone like me to do His will and work.

Your love for Jesus and your joy in Him is contagious. I know this firsthand. What is the most important fact to know about Him? What is the first thing you tell people about Him?

Jesus loves them, wants nothing but good for them. He died for them, He forgives them. It brings me great joy when people receive their salvation and the power He gives us through his Holy Spirit, knowing that nothing is impossible with Him.

There are so many sleeping sheep, do you try to awaken them? How?

No, I do not. I continuously talk about my Savior but if His Spirit is not drawing them, then neither am I.

Knowing the glory of God firsthand, you walk in unearthly confidence. How do you know He is with you all the time?

The Word of God says, "I will never leave you nor forsake you, and I will be with you even to the ends of the world." I believe it.

Please describe what happened to you after you were filled with the Holy Spirit. How did you respond to clergy and congregants from churches that you saw after you were born again, who treated you so poorly?

After I was filled with the Holy Spirit, I became an on-fire-for-Christ woman, I couldn't read or pray or study enough. I had to devour the word of God, asking who, what, where, and why. When I went to different churches, I was treated extremely badly because they only knew me by my worldly reputation.

You began walking in the gifts of healings and saw miracles right away. What is the difference between a healing and a miracle?

A healing takes time; a miracle, like what you had, is immediate. (Note: In 2015, God miraculously straightened the Interviewer's spine instantly after Vickie laid her hands on her back, praying for healing.)

After Jesus appeared to you and you were healed, you attended many more revivals. Who have you gotten to know, who have you influenced along the way? Who has influenced you? I know you have influenced so many people. Can you think of any persons in particular?

I spoke at the revivals. Derek Prince, Rick Renner, Joe and Linda Knight, Al Houghton, Winston Lynch (preaches in over 120 countries), the Wilkerson brothers, Leila Cost, and others. None of them had an influence on my life. We just became good friends. When they needed someone who walked in miracles, they called me. I remain close to this day to Brother Houghton and Brother Lynch.

You authored the Systematic Theology Syllabus used extensively by disciples to this day. How long did it take you to write it? Who uses it to this day and in what countries?

It took me 2-1/2 years to write the syllabus. Rick Renner used it all through Russia, Jose Murillo uses it in Latin America. It's used in South Korea, Brazil, and Mexico.

There are so many "posers" and "wanna-bes." What are red flags for you to steer away from charlatans?

I move very heavily in the gift of discernment. I know true Christians. If you just preach money, then mammon is your god. If you're "Jesus only," then you have forgotten God and the Holy Spirit. If you say it's OK to be gay, then stay away. Jesus warned us, in His word, there would be imposters, and I stay away from them. I don't give them the time of day. You can't change a fool's mind.

Your husband and your sister Celeste have been integral persons in protecting you and traveling with you. Please describe them and their part in the ministry.

My husband is an incredible man of God in my eyes. He has supported me through 53 nations; he paid my way, not the church. He is the one who caused me to preach the gospel. On a Sunday morning, years ago, he said he wasn't going to go to church. I said I am not going either. We put on our hip waders and fish vests. I put my fishing pole in his truck, and he drove me straight to the church. We both got out of the truck while I was telling him if he wasn't going why should I? He yelled back at me, "God called you to preach!" and he kept pushing me toward the door. I fell down. He picked me up, pushed me into the place where I was supposed to preach, and I am so thankful he did. There were people who came from the Kenai River, I was singing in the Spirit, and they came in and heard me speaking in German [Interviewer's note: Vickie does not speak German]. *At that time, one of the people said I had a greater ministry than Katherine Kuhlman; that God would send me around the world, and he said it in perfect English. My sister Celeste has always been the quiet steady rock in my life. Before I was born again, I wouldn't speak (because of shyness), I had to be high or drunk to say hello. She would do all the talking. After receiving salvation, you couldn't shut me up, and she quit talking. They both support me with everything they have, especially my husband, in whatever God would have me do. The odd thing, the strange thing is, they never question me.*

Do you hear God's voice? How often? Speaking of voices, please explain the gift of tongues. Yours sounds beautifully Spanish/ Portuguese to me. Mine sounds French/Arabic. Tell us more about this gift, please.

The word of God tells us, "My children will hear my voice and obey." I find true obedience is much better than sacrifice. Whenever God wants me to do something, He lets me know. The gift of tongues is a language unknown to me. Some even speak the language of angels; there are over 2000 languages, I do not know what mine is. I pray in tongues, and it brings great peace to my soul. I believe all believers should be baptized in the Spirit to receive the gift of tongues otherwise they are powerless. Jesus said stay here until you are endowed with power from on high. His Spirit helps me fight my flesh and keeps me from flagrant sin.

Please describe fasting and the fruits of fasting.

Fasting is an honor; you just stop eating and start drinking water. That is a true fast. It's no different than Moses going up the mountain for 40 days. I have done many fasts. Fasting helps to shut down your soul, so that you may hear the voice of God more plainly. A lot of people call Daniel's diet a fast, but it's not a fast, it's a diet. Fasting is literally not eating and just drinking water. There's no limitation on days, it's up to the individual. You will hit a hard spot, hunger spots, but you pray through them and drink more water. It is a powerful tool to help cast out demons.

When did you realize you walk in the Spiritual gift of healings and miracles?

I realized as soon as I read Mark 16; even though I was a baby in Christ, I believed it. I spoke in new tongues like it says, I battled demons in His name, so I started praying for the sick. I thought all Christians did it. The Bible said these signs will follow those who believe. Miracles, signs, and wonders are for the believers. We see them in our church all the time, including raising the dead.

The prayer you said when the Holy Spirit worked through your hands to heal my back was great. Do you remember it? Is there a prayer of Thanksgiving and praise you usually say? Verses in Scripture?

I said, "Jesus, please touch my sister through the power of the Holy Spirit, so that she will not end up looking like Quasimodo. I am asking in the name of You, Lord, to heal her now." As your back twisted, popped, and turned you sat there wide eyed just looking at me. The whole day you kept asking me to pray over your spine

because it felt so good. Psalm 91, Isaiah 43, and the Our Father.
[Note: Yes, Vickie actually said I was going to end up looking
like Quasimodo without God's divine intervention. Vickie has a
marvelous sense of humor, and God's timing is always perfect.]

**God works through you, the Holy Spirit is so obvious in you! What
was the first healing/miracle you remember being a part of? Please
tell us about some of the hundreds of healings and miracles you've
been blessed to participate in.**

*I was home talking to an elderly gentleman who had come to my
prayer meeting that I had every day. I called his wife and asked her
to come; she asked him to join her. He decided he could give God 30
minutes and came down. Our prayer time usually lasted 6 to 8 hours.
During prayer time, he let out a yell, God loosened his hip bones and
grew his leg about four inches. He should have died in Prudhoe Bay
when crushed by iron. Healed, he ran through the community for
days, he outran his own sons. People in the community tried to tell
him it wouldn't last. He is still doing great, but those who mocked and
ridiculed him are dead.*

**God always has a way of surprising us and stunning us with His glory!
What is the most extraordinary healing you have been a part of?**

*One evening coming home from work during winter, a young man
named Steven had flipped his car several times on the ice. The car
went down the embankment, I got there the same time the police did.
I grabbed his head as the cops got there. He gave a death gurgle. I
yelled, "In the name of Jesus come back to your body!" and you could
hear him inhale his Spirit. God told me he wasn't alone. I tried to tell
the police, but they wouldn't listen. They got Steven out from under his
vehicle but never searched for another person. The next day, the police
came to my door and asked, "How did I know" he wasn't alone. I told
them, "I told you – God told me, but you wouldn't listen even though
you claim to be a Christian. There was a young woman who had
struggled in the cold winter night for 8 hours before she died" Shame
on them who claimed to know God but never listen.*

Part of healing this world we're in is sharing His Gospel. How many works/ministries has God used you to start? What parts of the world? Over what period of time?

In 40 years, we have opened feeding programs, schools, churches, church camps, and missionary centers. We have done this throughout Africa, Central and South America, Asia and in Mexico. Whatever nation I go to, I start a new work of some sort because it is an honor to be trusted by our Most High God in that way.

Please describe the similarities and differences in the ministries in Africa and here in the United States.

In Africa, they have no money, no Social Security, no unemployment benefits. Families take care of families. The old are not put in nursing homes, they are taken care of by their families. They have few doctors; many children die of malaria. Kibera is the largest slum in Nairobi, and the largest urban slum in Africa. It has over 2 million homeless people, no sewage, no running water, no electricity. We started a school every day; we fed them every day with enough to take home. In the United States, we spoil our kids rotten. We have everything at an arm's reach, and when God takes it away, I pity the USA. Truly, I pity it; they have no idea what they are in for...so many people believe in the rapture, and yes, I find a few verses on it. However, the Book of Revelation says a little different story than what many are believing. Africa is on fire for God. America is lukewarm. Yes, there are many churches, pockets of true believers, but when He calls the remnant, the Ministries of the Living Stones truly is a remnant of God.

What did Jesus mean by "Upon this rock I will build my church"? Who holds the keys to the Kingdom?

Revelation. Knowledge of God. The keys are held by us through Jesus Christ.

What is the most important thing you want anyone to know?

The most important thing is to know Jesus Christ as your personal Savior; to be baptized in water and baptized in the Spirit (John 3:5), to be able to walk in His power as described in Mark 16:15-20. It makes me rather angry that there are so many religious sects out there who are Pharisees and Sadducees, who talk against my friend the Holy Ghost. I know what it means to be bought and paid for, as I worked in a brothel. It is easy for me to understand that I am bought by the sinless blood of a miraculous Savior.

How do you want to be remembered?

Handmaiden of the Lord. As a great woman of true faith.

What has been your biggest joy in life? Biggest sorrow? I know these are very personal questions, and I understand if you decide not to answer.

Salvation and knowing that Jesus is my big brother. The gift of the Holy Spirit that dwells within me. My biggest sorrow is that I didn't know Him sooner.

What is your absolute most favorite verse in Scripture?

Mark 16:15-20, Psalm 91, Isaiah 43

Chapter Eight

Miracles Around the World, Witnesses in the Philippines

But those who wait on the Lord
Shall renew their strength;

They shall mount up with wings like eagles,
They shall run and not be weary,
They shall walk and not faint.

Isaiah 40:31

God sent Vickie to places near and far. He had lovingly assigned to her His simple task, the same task He assigns to each and every one of His followers to this day:

Then the eleven disciples went away into Galilee,
to the mountain which Jesus had appointed for them.
When they saw Him, they worshiped Him; but some doubted.
And Jesus came and spoke to them, saying,
"All authority has been given to Me in heaven and on earth.
Go therefore and make disciples of all the nations,
baptizing them in the name of the Father and of the Son and of the
Holy Spirit,
teaching them to observe all things that I have commanded you;
and lo, I am with you always, even to the end of the age"
Matthew 28:16-20

~~~

Tell, baptize, and teach (Matthew 28:16-20). Vickie went wherever God led her.

She witnessed men and women giving their lives to Jesus, thousands of healings and miracles; the power of the Holy Ghost traveled with her wherever she went, meeting people where ever they were in life.

Clearly, she belonged to Him, and still does to this day. Vickie was no longer her own. When Jesus proclaimed to her, "You are mine." everything changed, she came to know

everything she ever knew in life up to that point was false, just as He had told her.

"He who is faithful in what is least is faithful also in much;
and he who is unjust in what is least is unjust also in much.
Therefore, if you have not been faithful in the unrighteous mammon,
who will commit to your trust the true riches?
And if you have not been faithful in what is another man's,
who will give you what is your own?
"No servant can serve two masters;
for either he will hate the one and love the other,
or else he will be loyal to the one and despise the other.
You cannot serve God and mammon."
Luke 16:10-13

Word traveled fast about the tall woman with the red hair who walked in the power of the Holy Spirit. People greeted her, clamoring to meet her wherever she went. She always, always praised God and gave Him all of the credit for everything.

"Out of the abundance of the heart, much is given," Vickie often says. Vickie loves God above all; God pours His grace generously on her.

~~~

Vickie vividly describes a few miraculous events she experienced in her travels:

"I had never put a fleece before the Lord; I have always just walked knowing God will do what He says, lay hands on the sick and they will be healed.

My husband wanted me to move to Nigeria; I was in Kenya at the time.

I did not want to move to Africa.

I prayed to God, 'Please, You have to tell me where to live, I don't want to leave the church You built. ...You have to show me where You want me.'

90

The tears ran down my face, I was outside screaming at the wind.

We had to travel to another town, driving in 100-degree weather, when we got the sign that said we entered the equator.

It started to snow and snowed until we left the equator.

I knew that was my answer.

The men who were driving stared at me like I was a crazy woman.

God changed my husband's heart, and we didn't move to Nigeria.

We traveled back to Alaska and continued to call it our home."

~ ~ ~

Vickie tells of another miraculous event:

"It was my second trip to Mexico. We had built the brand-new church and parsonage. I didn't know they were suffering from a five-year drought. They were the headwaters for all of Durango. I went to pray for rain.

One of the men who travelled with me, who knew me from Alaska, asked me to not pray because he knew I walked in the power of the Holy Spirit.

He said, "Let me get my fruit off my trees, and then pray."

I honored his request.

Once the harvest was done, God said, "It rains on the just and the unjust, it sunshines on the just and unjust."

It began to rain.

It rained so hard roofs collapsed.

There is a whole new lake there; they named it Lake Vickie. The Lord giveth and the Lord taketh away…they should have named it Lake Jesus.

~ ~ ~

Vickie has experienced several miracles during her journeys while sharing the gospel world-wide over the past 40 years. More recently, this Miracle happened in 2023 while Vickie was traveling together with an entourage of her students in the Philippines. Vickie tripped and was falling face first onto the cement while exiting a bus...here are some firsthand accounts from her students of what happened:

Jeana's Testimony

It was around 9 PM when Vickie and her team of 6 arrived via van transport from the airport to our destination for the evening, the Belmont Hotel in Manila. We all filed out of the van, and Vicki was one of the last to disembark.

As she stepped out of the van, her pink flip-flop caught on the step of the van and she started to pitch forward. I grabbed her right hand and tried to stop her from falling, but it was no use, she was falling forward headfirst toward the asphalt.

Somehow, only to be explained by God, Vickie's right knee bent, and she then started to fall backwards and alongside the bus. As we watched her fall, she floated to the ground, gently landing on her back with her left hand up in the air above her head. No one in the group could believe their eyes, Vickie was falling face-first but landed on her back as if she were a floating feather or a scene out of a movie, not even hitting her head on the ground which was a miracle.

We helped her up and proceeded to the hotel and up to our room. Vickie didn't have a scratch or bruise on her body from the fall.

Only by the grace of God and his angels watching over her did she remain unscathed and intact. The angels did indeed take charge that evening. Psalm 91:11-12 comes to mind:

> *For He shall give His angels charge over you,*
> *To keep you in all your ways.*
> *In their hands they shall bear you up,*
> *Lest you dash your foot against a stone.*

Dominique's Testimony

Seven of us rode in a bus to get to the hotel where we were staying, Vickie sat in the back of the bus with me. We were the last to get out. There were already people within our group that had gotten out who were waiting for the luggage to be unloaded. Vickie was closest to the door, so she was exiting ahead of me. I saw her trip. Her flip-flop had gotten caught on something and she could not catch her footing in time. It looked as though she was heading face-first into the cement ground.

Before anyone could react or even panic, as if I was watching a slow-motion film, I watched Vickie, whose back was originally facing me, in the air to be completely turned around. I watched her land ever so gently on the ground, facing me.

It was as if someone not only turned her over, but also slowed down her fall. Imagine dropping a feather five feet from the ground and watching it float to the ground. Immediately I knew she was alright.

After her reassurance that she was okay, I couldn't help but replay what I had seen in my head and laugh! I watched a miracle! She was falling face-first from five feet above the cement, and landed softly, on her back, completely unharmed.

I was watching Psalm 91:11-12 in action!

God was watching over us, and no one could deny it.

Nicki's Testimony

I turned around and saw Vickie falling forward very slowly with one foot forward outside of the van as if she had begun to step out. She was falling so slowly there was not a sense of alarm, rather, almost a sense of peace, like there wasn't anything to worry about, that the situation was under control.

I wasn't sure whether to take what I was seeing seriously and considered whether what I was seeing was a joke because it was so surreal. There was a complete absence of danger.

I remember thinking, "What great control that must take to move so slowly on a downward motion, only someone who is a dancer would know how much strength it would take to lower oneself down with such control and lack of speed."

I continued to watch Vickie falling slowly. I didn't move to help her but watched because, again, I wasn't sure what was happening. I knew it didn't involve me and there was no place for me to rush into the situation. As Vicki continued to fall slowly forward, I saw her body turn so that she wasn't going face-forward anymore but was lowered, or guided, to the ground on her side. She settled gently on to her back with one hand up against her forehead.

Janine's Testimony

I saw God protect Vickie. As Vickie was exiting a van, her foot got caught. She was falling forward headfirst, and then in slow motion, she was turned and was gently lowered to the ground. What should have been a hard fall, she was being guided gently to the ground. This all happened in slow motion; that is the only way to describe what happened.

God protected her, gently guiding her to the ground. It was the protective hand of God stopping her from being seriously hurt. In fact, she had no injuries at all.

Sierra's Testimony

On the last leg of our journey to the Philippines, we finally arrived in Manila. Eager to get checked into our hotel, we started climbing out of the two airport limousine vans, unloading luggage, putting our items through the security line. There were still some people getting out of the van behind me when I heard one of the girls behind Vickie in the van yell out.

I turned, and out of my peripheral vision I saw Vickie falling forward out of the van descending headfirst towards the cobblestone and curbed edge. I turned and stepped attempting to catch her, but I knew I wasn't going to be fast enough, she was just out of reach.

Something strange happened at that moment.

As she started to fall forward, midair, it was as if an invisible force slowed time, picked her up, turned her around, and laid her down. She appeared to *float to the ground like a feather*, transformed from a stumbling forward into the most graceful and soft fall I had ever seen.

I had got to her just in time to grab her head, but there was no weight to it, no momentum, no force. She defied gravity, there was nothing to hold or to catch.

We all stood there, kind of stunned, and kept asking if she was okay.

She said she was fine; her flip-flop had caught the sidestep of the van as she was exiting the vehicle, tripping her and propelling her forward. She didn't have a scratch on her, and she kept giggling there was nothing wrong.

Dominique chimed in, "That was the most graceful tumble I've ever seen in my life," and we all laughed in agreement, not sure what we had just witnessed, but knowing it was not natural, and our leader, by all laws of nature, should have been injured.

As I thought back at this moment in the following weeks after our trip, I found myself asking God what exactly He had done. I was reminded of the verse, "He shall give his angels charge over you, to keep you in all your ways. In their hands they shall bear you up, lest you dash your foot against a stone" (Psalm 91:11-12). The entire psalm is about how when you abide in God's presence, make Him your refuge, your dwelling place, and set your love upon Him, that He keeps you, delivers you, and is with you in your time of trouble.

I witnessed the promise of divine protection by the Divine Keeper in action that day.

I saw what I now know was an angel pick Vickie up, turn her around, and set her down so that she did not as so much dash her foot or head against a stone.

Kalee's Testimony

Vickie and her team were traveling for mission work in the

Philippines. I had the privilege to be one of those members and got to witness many miraculous moments in Jesus Christ. One of those incredible moments was while travelling to Manila.

We were all loaded in a van and were headed to our next destination. The driver opened the door, motioning for Vickie to step out. I was sitting behind her in the back and could see her falling to the pavement.

She is mature in age which caused sudden panic to set in. I was worried that she would seriously injure herself as it was a large van she was falling out of. Her flip-flop caught the edge of the door, she was headed face-first for the ground.

But something odd happened...she didn't fly face-first into the cement. She floated. I physically saw her gently flutter to the ground and land on her back. It was almost as if there was a pillow underneath her and a hand gently laid her down. She didn't hit her face; she didn't injure her body.

My worry quickly dissipated, and we all began to laugh with relief. I couldn't believe my eyes! I saw her flying headfirst out of the van, and there she was, lying there as if nothing happened. No injury, no pain, and no issues.

I know God caught her. His angels had to have been there. It wasn't an ordinary occurrence; it was a supernatural moment. Vickie experienced a physical miracle in front of our eyes, and no one could deny what an awesome thing God had just done. He protected her from any harm.

I believe she still has work to do and another job to accomplish. She might be mature in years, but there is still a plan for her life. Nothing was going to come in between her health and the task set before her and us.

This woman is a dynamic person, teaching the next generation. She was opening the doors to nations with us because God had graced her to do so. God's grace gently laid her down on the sidewalk that day. I will never forget the Miracle I saw that day.

I was reminded of these verses in Isaiah:

He gives power to the weak,
And to those who have no might He increases strength.
Even the youths shall faint and be weary,
And the young men shall utterly fall,
But those who wait on the Lord shall renew their strength;

They shall mount up with wings like eagles,
They shall run and not be weary,
They shall walk and not faint.

Isaiah 40:29-31

Chapter Nine

Baptism in the Holy Spirit

"And as I began to speak, the Holy Spirit fell upon them

just as it had upon us at the beginning.

And I remembered the word of the Lord,

how he had said,

'John baptized with water, but you will be baptized with the Holy
Spirit.'"

Acts 11:15-16

"The Holy Spirit is omnipotent and ubiquitous; He is my best friend," Vickie says. She adds, "I don't deserve Him, but He stays with me anyway."

Vickie will tell you, "Since the Holy Spirit is the very Spirit of God, He always was and always will be. When He created us, He gave us the gift of free will. We have the blessed opportunity to decide to invite His Holy Spirit into our lives. When we make that decision to accept His Holy Gift to us, when we invite the Holy Spirit into our life through Baptism in the Spirit, extraordinary changes occur."

~~~

When people think of baptism, they generally think only about Baptism by Water (Romans 3:23-24; Mark 1:4-5; Acts 8:12; 36-38), most do not even know about Baptism in the Spirit.

John the Baptist had this to say about Baptism in the Holy Spirit: "I baptize you with water for repentance, but one who is more powerful than I is coming after me; I am not worthy to carry his sandals. He will baptize you with the Holy Spirit and fire" (Matthew 3:11). Of course, he is referring to the ministry works of the coming Messiah.

The Apostle John, records the words of John the Baptist as the one who spoke of the person who will "baptize with the Holy Spirit." "I myself did not know him, but the one who sent me to baptize with water said to me, 'He on whom you see the Spirit descend and remain is the one who baptizes with the Holy Spirit'" (John 1:33).

The only recorded time Jesus Christ used the phrase is found in the Book of Acts. Before His ascension into heaven, Jesus said to His disciples, "John baptized with water, but in just a few days you will be baptized with the Holy Spirit" (Acts 1:5).

Vickie explains, "Baptism by water is separate; baptism in the Holy Spirit completes sanctification and allows you to walk in His power, according to God's plan for you and His creation."

~~~

Vickie describes her Baptism in the Holy Spirit on July 4th, 1982:

Our Bible tells us that he who believes and is baptized will be saved. Jesus told us to follow Him, and He said that we would do greater things than He had done (John 14:12).

The Book of Acts tells us about the twelve in the Upper Room that were left in one heart, one mind, one accord. They heard the mighty wind of God blowing through and saw "the tongues of fire" dancing on each one's head (Acts 2:3).

The Bible tells us this gift is for every man, woman and child from generation to generations. Who am I to disagree with it?

When I stood up to be baptized with the Holy Spirit they told me to sit down. The preacher kept preaching about the gift. The congregation told me to sit down and hush. The third time I stood up, I turned to the congregation and asked how many wanted this gift from God.

I am quite bold. Nineteen other people stood up, so I put my arm out and said, "Give me the gift," knowing nothing from God will hurt me, "I don't need to understand it, I need to accept it."

There are many scriptures in the Bible, and it's the Father and the Son who we ask to fill us with the precious Holy Spirit. I view the Word of God very simply yet deeply. The Trinity: God thinks it, Jesus speaks it and the Holy Spirit does it.

~~~

Vickie teaches how by being baptized in the Holy Spirit, "We receive the perfect amount of grace to open heaven's door, just enough to allow His Holy Light to shine on us, shedding perfect amounts of wisdom and understanding according to His will for us. There are holy times when it's enough to actually witness His Holy Magnificence, other times to feel spiritually sturdy enough to humbly ask for forgiveness when the mere thought of it, otherwise, would be impossible."

Vickie refers to the scripture verse that tells us that it is when we are at our weakest that He is the strongest for us (2 Corinthians 12:10).

Then, there are those amazing times when He hands us the keys, through the power of this holy baptism, to unlock the doors of Heaven's Heart to be able to alleviate the suffering of others. Through Him, we are able to lay hands on the sick to heal them, and even to bring the dead back to life. "With Him we can do marvelous things; without Him we cannot do a single thing," she says.

There are other times when we know, we truly know, exactly what to say because God has replaced our words with His Words. He loves us so very much. "If people knew the Power He is willing to make available to us through Him, they would fall over," Vickie says, and there are times she has seen them do just that.

Our Lord God Almighty lets us into His Holy Place with even just a smidgeon of faith (Matthew 13:31-32), the exact amount we need, according to Him, to be able to eke out a holy life on this earth; enough so we can spend eternity with Him.

We come to know the Power of Father God, the Love of Jesus Christ, His beloved Son, and the Creation and Comfort of His Holy Spirit.

His Holy Word tells us,

> *"Now concerning spiritual gifts, brothers and sisters,*
> *I do not want you to be unaware.*
> *You know that when you were pagans,*

you were led astray to the mute idols,
however, you were led.
Therefore, I make known to you that no one speaking by the Spirit of
God says,
"Jesus is accursed"; and no one can say, "Jesus is Lord,"
except by the Holy Spirit.
Now there are varieties of gifts, but the same Spirit.
And there are varieties of ministries, and the same Lord.
There are varieties of effects,
but the same God who works all things in all persons.
But to each one is given the manifestation of the Spirit for the common
good.
For to one is given the word of wisdom through the Spirit,
and to another the word of knowledge according to the same Spirit;
to another faith by the same Spirit,
and to another gifts of healing by the one Spirit,
and to another the effecting of miracles,
and to another prophecy, and to another the distinguishing of spirits,
to another various kinds of tongues, and to another the interpretation
of tongues.
But one and the same Spirit works all these things,
distributing to each one individually just as He wills.
For just as the body is one and yet has many parts,
and all the parts of the body,
though they are many, are one body, so also is Christ.
For by one Spirit we were all baptized into one body, whether Jews or
Greeks, whether slaves or free, and we were all made to drink of one
Spirit.
1 Corinthians 12:1-13

Now you are Christ's body, and individually parts of it.
And God has appointed in the church,
first apostles, second prophets, third teachers,
then miracles, then gifts of healings,
helps, administrations, and various kinds of tongues.
All are not apostles, are they? All are not prophets, are they?
All are not teachers, are they?
All are not workers of miracles, are they?
All do not have gifts of healings, do they?
All do not speak with tongues, do they?
All do not interpret, do they?
But earnestly desire the greater gifts.
1 Corinthians 12:27-31

Why do organized religions not tell us about His powerful, holy, and sacred gift?

Vickie explains the reason is two-fold, "First, the spirit of religion is corrupt. It's demonic (2 Corinthians 11:13-14). It is self-centered and self-serving. Jesus loathed the Pharisees and anyone who puffed themselves up pretending to be holier-than-thou. Modern day churches are cringe-worthy with their entertainment, pastors in the pulpit tickling ears with putrid garbage to keep them sticking around so their church "businesses" flourish. They are foul. "Fools find no pleasure in understanding but delight in airing their own opinions" (Proverbs 18:2).

"'Religion' does not possess the Holy Spirit of God," Vickie explains. "Their corrupt leaders want you to believe they are holding the keys to the kingdom; they want us to think we have to go through them and their garbage to get to God. They lie. God, seeing our unworthiness and loving us anyway, is handing His keys directly to each one of us."

Vickie recalls, "If God Himself can save my filthy self, lying in a brothel with a .357 in my mouth, He surely can save you, too!"

Vickie says one of the most important conversations to have with our Lord God is this: "Please expose me to myself for Your Glory so I can work on what is wrong with me."

Secondly, Vickie says, "Many just plain do not know. They do not read His Word, and if they do read it, then they are spirit-less and just plain don't trust Him."

"The religious spirit destroys – just look at the major religions of the world. They all suppress and abuse women," Vickie says, having experienced this firsthand.

Romans 16:17 is specific, "Now I urge you, brethren, note those who cause divisions and offenses, contrary to the doctrine which you learned, and avoid them. For those who are such do not serve our Lord Jesus Christ, but their own belly, and by smooth words and flattering speech deceive the hearts of the simple."

~~~

Vickie teaches, from her firsthand Holy Spirit-led experiences, how to recognize the deceptive illusion of a demonic spirit of religion.

This passage describes it well:

Recognize the Deceptive Illusion of a Religious Spirit:

Avoid Its Influence. Religious spirits have a form of godliness. We are instructed by the Apostle Paul, "From such turn away." Religious spirits spend a great deal of time talking about what great and magnificent things they are going to do for God, yet seldom do more than criticize others. With an understanding of the evil designs of the religious spirit, it becomes vital to recognize its characteristics so we can turn away from its influence.

In a letter to Timothy, the Apostle Paul warns his spiritual son about religious spirits and gives him implicit instructions about how to interact with them. Scripture says, "Having a form of godliness, but denying the power thereof: from such turn away" (2 Timothy 3:5). As Paul so matter-of-factly points out, religious spirits have a "form of godliness" – they appear religious but lack the spiritual substance of an intimate believer. Paul told Timothy to avoid such people – and with good reason. Religious spirits sidetrack people with the deceptive illusion of religious form. Religious form is this: Appearance, Structure, Ceremony, Formula, Liturgy, Ritual.

More interested in liturgy than liberty, religious spirits are focused on outward appearances. Religious spirits look at things like the church building, the size of the congregation, where the church is located, and who is attending to decide whether or not they want to be a member of the assembly. They are more interested in form than what the Spirit of God is doing among the people. The result is that they miss the spiritual dynamics of the church because of a focus on carnal externals.[8]

~~~

Conversely, this is what Jesus says about His Church:

Jesus emphasized love and unity among believers as being central to the mission of the church. He prayed that his followers "may all be one" just as He and the Father are one (John 17:21). This oneness comes through the Holy Spirit who enables believers to love one another just as Jesus loved them (John 13:34-35).

Such love and unity enable the church to reveal God's love to the world and testify that Jesus was sent by God (John 17:23).

Paul also stressed the importance of unity, exhorting believers to live in harmony, be sympathetic, love one another, and look not only to their own interests but also to the interests of others (Philippians 2:2-4).

He implored the Corinthians that there be no divisions among them but that they be united in the same mind and judgment (1 Corinthians 1:10).

Therefore, love and unity are essential to the church fulfilling its God-given mission. Petty divisions, selfish ambition, and lack of love undermine the church's witness. As Jesus said, this visible love and unity testify to the world of His love and the truth of His identity as the Son sent from the Father (John 17:21, 23).

Jesus demonstrated that greatness in His kingdom is attained through servanthood and humility rather than domineering authority. He washed His disciples' feet, presenting Himself as an example for them to follow, humbly serving one another (John 13:1-17).

He taught that the first will be last and the last first (Mark 9:35). He instructed His followers not to lord authority over others as the Gentiles do but to serve one another in humility (Matthew 20:25-28).

The early church embodied this spirit of mutual service. Believers shared meals, supported those in need, and used their gifts to build up others (Acts 2:42-47). Leaders were to be examples to the flock, not domineering over it but proving themselves humble servants (1 Peter 5:1-5).

Paul echoed Christ's teaching that each member should look not only to his own interests but also to the interests of others (Philippians 2:4).

Therefore, the church is called to follow Jesus' model of humble, selfless service toward one another. Pride and selfish ambition have no place. As each member serves others in humility and love, the church functions as a unified community of believers.[9]

~~~

God has used Vickie to start hundreds of missions world-wide. Vickie won't tell you this, though. She will tell you her name is not on anything except her utility bill in Alaska.

She always says, "It's not about me. Why would I put my name on it? Everything is for His Glory, for the building of His Kingdom. Everything. It's not about me. Who am I? Without Him, I am nothing.

We learn to trust Him. We trust Him with our life, our death, and everything in between.

Vickie knows this.

But the Helper, the Holy Spirit,
whom the Father will send in My name,
He will teach you all things,
and bring to your remembrance all things that I said to you.
John 14:26

Chapter Ten

Teach Me

'Not by might nor by power, but by My Spirit,'
Says the Lord of hosts.

Zechariah 4:6

"God has blessed me through every one of you here," Vickie says at the start of a service at Ministry of the Living Stones. Her presence is huge, larger than life. You can feel the power of Holy Spirit in the room. The love for each other is tangible, the genuine warmth is comforting. Every person there wants to be there, there are no slackers. This is the place to be for replenishment, refreshment, rejuvenation in the Spirit. This is a place of worship. This place is holy. It is crowded. It is Wednesday night.

"Rejoice in what you have, it's all from Christ. Every single bit of it," she says, arms outstretched.

"Open your Bibles to Luke 17:11-19," she says, calling on Dominique to, "Preach it, don't teach it! I don't need to know what it says. Preach it!"

Barefoot, and oh-so-obviously filled with His Holy Spirit, the young woman opens her mouth in praise saying, "Father, I ask that You anoint this Word and every mouth that speaks it, that You would anoint the Word, that you would anoint the hearts to receive it and the ears to hear it. We thank You for this opportunity in Jesus' mighty name. Amen."

She takes a deep breath, looking up. She is glowing. There is peace and safety beyond understanding in the room.

She begins by reading the verses in Luke, when Vickie gently directs her to close her Bible and preach from her heart. "We all know what it says," Vickie says, "preach to us what it means."

"When you have an encounter with Jesus," Dominique smiles, "everything changes."

She knows. Her body was miraculously healed years ago. Then, His Spirit led her to know how true healing from God works from the inside – out. "Thank You, Lord," she says, "thank You, I need You more than just for the healing of my body, I need You every day to live in my heart."

"A few years ago," she says, "I had nothing. Absolutely nothing." God called her, she answered Him.

"He wants your heart," she knows, "if He has to strip you of everything you have and everyone you know, He will," she says, "it takes humility to admit we need Him for everything."

"There is no room for self-righteousness in His Kingdom. You cannot busily build your own kingdom and then put His name on it. It won't work. It will not end well for you. I know this firsthand," she says. "He will heal you on the outside; you need to be healed on the inside, too."

"I had to get rid of all of the idols in my life; all of the things I thought were important. He showed me what my idols were," she admits, "He allowed me to be the one leper who was healed out of the ten, the one who came back to Him to say, 'Thank You for healing me Lord,' when the other nine never returned to say thanks."

"The other lepers were healed on the outside; their hearts remained the same. The leper who came back to thank Jesus was grateful. His heart was filled with gratitude and humility. He realized Jesus was not only the Great Healer, but He was also his Savior."

"When we have an encounter with God, there's more than just a healing waiting for us, there's more than that. There's more than what we are searching for with our eyes. When we are open and willing and have a true encounter with Jesus, our heart is transformed. Allow God to change you from the inside out!"

Now, *that* is the way to teach how to preach, and this is what Vickie has been teaching for over 40 years. "Let the Holy Spirit work through you!"

~~~

Vickie teaches those souls with whom she has been entrusted, the ones God put in her life. When Dominque was finished preaching, Vickie reminded everyone to, "Remember where we came from. Know why we are here. Stay right with the King, He has a divine purpose for our lives, we belong to Him."

He is with her. She knows this, He is right there with them all.

The Holy Spirit works through Vickie in a supernatural way. She works tirelessly inspiring those around her to become interested in their own salvation, to actively participate in their own restoration through Him. She teaches them how to teach others, she shows them how to preach His Word.

She will tell you, "There are times and seasons for everything. God considers what the world considers as trash, cleans it up, and uses it. I was of this world; God is miraculous in everything He does. If He can flip my life, He can flip anyone's life."

Vickie reminds us, "Nothing comes to you without God's permission to teach you. Religion has no power. Only God can save you. Seek His Truth. Ask, 'How do I get there?'"

"Your responsibilities will be great but not as great as your possibilities," she says, "the higher He brings you, the lower you must submit to Him. To walk in great power, you have to come to a place of great brokenness requiring full surrender."

"The closer we come to the Lord, the more we must die. We lay down our lives to where Jesus is Lord over us. Become open and willing to allow the Holy Spirit to expose what God wants to change in you so that God can use you for His honor and glory. Trust Him. Anything that has great value will come at a great price. Die to self, God's will be done."

"He brings us to a place where we submit to one another. Stand with a person in their suffering and lead them to that holy place of faith. Train their eyes on Jesus! Not you, not their pain. The whole purpose is to glorify God. Who are we serving? It is a blessing to be a part of the building of the body of Christ. The goal is always to get one's eyes on Jesus."

~~~

Vickie knows deep sadness and pain. Her name has been dragged through the garbage pit by the enemy, she has been gossiped about and has had many threats on her life since Jesus saved her that day in the bordello.

How does she cope?

Miraculously, she forgives them.

"Thinking you can hurt me by bringing up my past is like trying to rob my old house. I don't live there anymore," she says.

"Forgive them who spitefully use you," she says, "Jesus forgave them, He showed us, He taught us how to forgive. We are told, 'We are forgiven according to how we forgive.'"

But I say to you who hear: Love your enemies, do good to those who hate you,

bless those who curse you and pray for those who spitefully use you.

To him who strikes you on the one cheek, offer the other also.

And from him who takes away your cloak, do not withhold your tunic either.

Give to everyone who asks of you.

And from him who takes away your goods do not ask them back.

And just as you want men to do to you, you also do to them likewise.

"But if you love those who love you, what credit is that to you?

For even sinners love those who love them.

And if you do good to those who do good to you, what credit is that to you?

For even sinners do the same.

And if you lend to those from whom you hope to receive back, what credit is that to you?

For even sinners lend to sinners to receive as much back.

But love your enemies, do good, and lend, hoping for nothing in return;

and your reward will be great, and you will be sons of the Most High.

For He is kind to the unthankful and evil.

Therefore, be merciful, just as your Father also is merciful.
Luke 6:27-36

"My sins are forgiven. Who am I to not forgive you?" she asks. "Yours will be too, ask Him for forgiveness. Change your ways – repent   and learn to stay away from evil. We do not return to the cesspool God delivered us from."

"His Word promises that if we seek Him, we will find Him. When we surrender our lives to Him, everything changes."

And do not be conformed to this world,
but be transformed by the renewing of your mind,
that you may prove what is that good
and acceptable and perfect will of God.
Romans 12:2

"You will be rejected, gossiped about, betrayed by those you love," she says. "Jesus was rejected, gossiped about, betrayed, too. Those are the deep wounds that do not show, the invisible drops of His precious blood of salvation on each one of us. These are the wounds we cannot see with our human eyes. He suffered all of these things; of course we will, too."

~~~

The men and women standing shoulder to shoulder in this holy place know their body is "the temple of the Holy Spirit" who is in them, whom they have from God, and they know they belong to Him.
"I will dwell in them
And walk among them.
I will be their God,
And they shall be My people."
2 Corinthians 6:16

Every person who gathers together there with their brothers and sisters in our Christ Jesus, gather together "as living stones, being built up a spiritual house, a holy priesthood, to offer up spiritual sacrifices acceptable to God through Jesus Christ" (1 Peter 2:5).

They have been taught to take that sanctuary with them in their hearts when they leave that place. They are temples of His Holy Spirit all the time, not just when they are there. They are called to be holy, and they know it.

Every person who has had the privilege of being taught by Vickie knows this, lives this, breathes these Truths. Their eyes are opened, they see people in need and minister to them. They feed the hungry, give clothing to those who need it, they shelter the homeless. Vickie has set the example, lived these holy orders, since the day Jesus appeared to her in the brothel.

They visit those in prison, lay hands on the sick, watching them recover by the power of God Himself, praising Him through it all.

Restore to me the joy of Your salvation,
And uphold me by Your generous Spirit.
Then I will teach transgressors Your ways,
And sinners shall be converted to You.
Psalm 51:12-13

~ ~ ~

"Sometimes I was rough; I knew I was not dealing with the person, I was dealing with the satanic forces behind that person that bind the afflicted," Vickie says. She knows firsthand when Jesus healed people he was freeing them from the oppression of the devil (Acts 10:38).

"When one of us hurts, we all hurt." Vickie knows.

"I can't stand to see people hurting," Vickie says. "I know what it's like, I know how it feels deep down inside to have your heart ripped out and shoved back in upside down. It's the most diabolical thing. We have to forgive."

"The religious in Jesus' day killed Him, the religious system in His time. He forgave them, 'Father, forgive them, for they do not know what they do'" (Luke 23:34).

"We must stay on guard against the workings of the enemy. A person gets weak from sitting still and doing nothing. Most churches today are doing nothing, they are not in the trenches. The complacency of the religious false systems was set up by the devil. Hypocrisy, lies, deceptions, and delusions keep the people sick – and unsaved."

"When we are dealing with the Truth, the Word of God, He is with us, and we overcome through Him. Fear is the opposite of faith. Faith is the meeting ground between your limited self and your limitless God. 'Say the word and my servant will be healed,' (Matthew 8:8).

When Jesus sent His Holy Spirit, He made the gifts and the fruits of God available to all who seek Him. We surrender to the fruit of the Spirit, not the fruit of the flesh.

"I see Light and I see dark. It's all Light to me because I get to pray for it. I am a blessed woman to be able to see it and pray for it."

~~~

"Lord, give them the revelation of who they are in You," is Vickie's silent prayer.

Vickie knows dying to one's old self, letting go of the pride, the idols, the selfishness, is the only way to open the door to receive God's salvation. After all, remember, she said the Sinner's Prayer for days during the revival before she was saved, and nothing happened.

She knows how for some, it will take going to the edge of life, like it did for her, for the Good Shepherd to rescue them. She says she would not wish the pain and suffering she went through on anyone.

How do you wake someone up to His mercy? She knows she cannot make anyone believe in Him. Faith is a gift, sitting right there in front of every person, waiting for their soul to want to open it. Jesus said, "Because you have seen Me, have you believed? Blessed are they who did not see, and yet believed" (John 20:29). After all, "now faith is the assurance of things hoped for, the conviction of things not seen" (Hebrews 11:1).

So, Vickie is His walking epistle of His love, she is His handmaiden in service to Him.

She knows she can trust Him, and she does.

~~~

Vickie knows most people like sin more than they love God. She also knows He will not operate from an unclean vessel; He will only operate through those who have been washed by the blood of Jesus.

"We are all sinners, we are all unworthy, what a blessed miracle for Him to love us anyway," she says.

Those who have surrendered their life to Him as she has, strive to be more like Him every day. Saved from ourselves, we want to serve Him, we want everyone we meet to know Him, to walk in His miraculous power, to alleviate the misery in others, just as He relieves it in us.

"Praise Him!" she teaches. "Praise Him in success, praise Him in failure, praise Him in every circumstance of your life! Nothing – absolutely nothing – happens without His permission."

"We learn to take responsibility for the decisions we make," Vickie reminds us, "we learn to do better. We intentionally get rid of the idols in our life, the things that separate us from God."

"The importance of praising God is mentioned thousands of times in the Bible, both in the Old and New Testaments," she says. "The angels constantly worship God (Isaiah 6:3, Revelation 4:8), so the devil most likely was the worship leader in heaven before being banished from there by God."

"You will get attacked by Satan when you praise God. Sing louder! Praise louder! Sing so loud you cannot hear any other thoughts except the praise you are singing to our Creator!" she emphatically tells us all.

~~~

"God's chosen dwelling place is with His people, 'Do you not know that you are the temple of God and that the Spirit of God dwells in you?'" (1 Corinthians 3:16-17), she says.
Vickie teaches through example, loving deeply, caring openly, trusting God to work powerfully through her.

It is important to note here, "Non-Spirit led men and some women, too, think they cannot learn anything from a woman, throwing insults in an attempt to silence her. Thankfully, the Holy Spirit's gifts of wisdom and knowledge cut through that nonsense. His Wisdom fills us with Truth. Our Creator never would silence half of His beautiful creation. Spiritually unsaved men and women will skew the Truth for their own benefit," Vickie says.

Every single word Vickie teaches is in agreement with God's Word (2 Timothy 2:15; 3:16-17; 4:2; Hebrews 4:12). "Jesus sent His Holy Spirit for us – the gifts and the fruits of God are available to all who seek Him," she tells us.

~~~

"The world is getting more dangerous as the days go by," Vickie observes, "my eyes can see, my ears can hear. Nothing is the same as it used to be. Things are perpetually changing for the worse. The Word of God never changes, it is a solid rock in my life, it should be a solid rock in everyone's life. You can trust God, you can trust Jesus, and you can trust the Holy Ghost. People will betray you, Jesus is the author and finisher, He called us, He chose us, He did a divine intervention, so He could take what the world considers garbage and if you truly trust Him – well, then greater than I have done, you will do. Trust and believe in Christ, the Bible, not what you see or hear."

"Allow the Lord of your life BE the Lord of your life!" Vickie exclaims.

Chapter Eleven

Second Interview With Vickie

Trust in the Lord with all your heart,
And lean not on your own understanding;
In all your ways acknowledge Him,
And He shall direct your paths.

Proverbs 3:5-6

If you could put a definition on "anointing," what would it be?

Anointing is the presence of God, the power of the Holy Spirit that overshadows you, leads you, fills your mouth according to the scripture you are preaching; without the presence of God, it is a dead service. It is the anointing, the Holy Spirit of God, that moves across the congregation, no matter how small or large, that transfers the Word from the speaker to the hearer. It is what makes the deaf hear and the lame walk. The anointing is a must for any ministry to be founded and to grow. The gift and call is without repentance, but the anointing must be tended to by seeking the Lord with fasting, prayer, and reading the Bible. Without the anointing, it is a soul work, it is a flesh work, it is a repetitive work. The Spirit of God keeps things fresh, and it always seems new to the hearer. The anointing is ever changing as we grow and mature.

In the beginning, how did people hear about you? How did the invitations happen? How were these trips funded?

I was preaching in Sterling and Anchorage; people were talking about the crazy lady that preached the word of God. They would tell their pastors, and one thing led to another. The Lord brought people into my life; I didn't want to leave my community.

Trips were funded by my husband. He has always stood beside me— like Priscilla and Aquila.

Please describe your husband's role/part in the Ministry and how it has evolved over the years. I know you defer to David, as his wife, how does this apply to the Ministry?

David is the backbone of everything I do. He built the church buildings and funded my work abroad. The greatest in God's kingdom serves. He has gone from being active physically to now mentoring young people in the church, teaching them that they can be more than conquerors. He isn't a religious man...he is a Christian man. He quit traveling with me in the late 90's when we went to a church in Escazu, Costa Rica. David really enjoyed the young pastoral couple. During a prayer meeting, after I had prayed, the people had fallen flat on their backs and were manifesting. He never travelled with me again.

Let's talk about "religion," please. Can you describe firsthand your experiences with religion? Non-denominational churches are just as religious as the denominations. They are all abominations. Please expand.

When my sister and I were born again, the word traveled quickly. Everyone knew who we were. Shortly after, we were approached by the presbyters of churches in Alaska, Washington, Oregon, Idaho, California...they wanted us to travel to their churches. We had talked to the five men; they were nice but very sad. They said to my sister and me, if we would travel to their churches, all we would have to do is wear our furs, makeup, jewelry, and give our testimony. I said we hadn't read the whole Bible yet, and they said it didn't matter because church was 90% show and 10% word. I said a few choice words to them and never went back.

You met Trombley, Trombley met you. Oh, how I would have loved to listen in on that meeting. What is the most memorable part of that meeting for you?

We ran into each other at the Hilton Inn for a conference. We were both speaking at the conference; little did I know we were speaking at the same place. I got to minister with Brother Trombly for the weekend, and he gave me his newly released book, Who Said Women Can't Teach.

You were approached to start a work in Bethlehem. How did that come about, and what happened?

I went to Israel; it must have been my eighth or nineth trip. I met a lot of influential people in Bethlehem, they invited myself and five pastors to come to dinner in Bethlehem. While we were having dinner, the host said he wanted to start a church. He pointed to me. "I want you to handle it, to build it, run it, preach in it. Give the people what you have, teach them what you know." I didn't make any commitment to him because the other pastors were getting upset that he hadn't asked them. He didn't want another religious system; he wanted the truth. He was an extremely wealthy, wealthy man. I told him I would call him from Alaska. I came home a few days later, and the phone was ringing. It was Washington, DC. They told me I couldn't build a church in Bethlehem. I don't know how they knew; one was an ambassador from Italy; one was known as the stealth evangelist. I was very upset that I was eavesdropped on. When you are busy about the things of God, everyone is watching you, waiting for you to fall. Don't give them what they want.

The Gifts of the Holy Spirit work freely through you. Knowledge, Wisdom, Faith, Healing, Miracles, Prophesy, Distinguishing between spirits, Tongues/Interpretation of tongues—I know there are so many you could list. Do any come to mind right away that you are willing to share the experience, please?

If you were the only person on an island that was a believing Christian, how many of these wonderful gifts would God have you move in? You would evangelize, prophesy, heal the sick, receive Words of Wisdom, Words of Knowledge. It is very, very simple when you trust in Christ, and if you are willing to be moved by the Spirit of God, He will use you. If you aren't prideful, God will use you in all these gifts according to His will for you.

Are you willing to share your experiences with imprecatory prayers?

I'll share yours, Luanne. I stayed at your home. I was fasting for 14 days, water only, when I got a Word of knowledge. I prayed an imprecatory prayer that God would send an earthquake to a town on the Kenai Peninsula to awaken the Christians, so they would come alive to the fact that He has total control over everything. No sooner had I said my prayer, within 5 minutes, there was a 7.3 earthquake. (Note: November 30, 2018, at 2:09 PM AKST, KBBI.org News reported: "Kenai Peninsula Communities Report Damage Following a 7.3 Earthquake.")

There are angels, and there are demons. Are you willing to share experiences you've had with both?

One time, while I was on a 40-day water only fast, I came home to find my house bone chilling cold. It was in the middle of winter, the heat was on, but no heat was coming out of the furnace. I turned on my gas oven and the four stove top burners, but no heat emanated from them. I went into my bedroom right next to the kitchen. I wrapped myself in an electric blanket and lay on my king size water bed. I started to roll over and thought my cockapoo Clementine was jumping at my face. It wasn't my dog Clementine, it was the demon over Sterling, Alaska. It had come to do battle with a child of God. When the Holy Spirit opened my eyes to discern, I saw a monstrous hand physically trying to suffocate me in my pillows. It paralyzed half of my face. Out of the other side of my mouth I was yelling the name of Jesus. The demon picked me up by the hips and shook me like a rag doll very rapidly and threw me into the ceiling. I hit the floor, and the demon hit my king-size waterbed and shoved it into my dresser, and the scarves and belts were standing up like cobras. I made my way to the telephone and called for help. I stood in the middle of the kitchen with my arms extended praying in tongues, and help arrived. Four friends came through my front door and began to anoint my home with oil while I continued praying in the Spirit with the gift of tongues. They made their way through my home anointing every open portal, window, and door. One of my friends, Fran, got hit in the face and literally went flying about 12 feet. She jumped up and yelled, "The perfect love of God casts out all fear!" and went back to the laundry room to complete anointing the room. The demon opened the front door and slammed it shut so hard it shook the whole house. The temperature went from 0° to 90° in a split second. This is one example; I have seen several more demonic events through my travels preaching the word of God. Angels, I have had the honor of seeing them with my naked eye. Sometimes as flashes of light, especially in the wintertime when it is dark. I have seen them hover over people, bringing gifts, ministering angels bringing gifts and leaving with them because the person's faith was not activated to receive. I have seen angels both in church and out of church.

Did you ever return to visit Eadie's Brothel? What happened?

No, I did go to her funeral. Once I left, I left. I won't be a dog returning to its vomit. However, I did go back when I was 65 years old to pray. It was no longer Eadie's as Eadie's but a mission for men needing the Lord. I wanted to go to where I was spiritually born. They had to unlock the room and let me in; the anointing was so tangible, they didn't let anyone in the room. They did open the room shortly after I was there visiting. A man was put in there and was delivered from alcoholism and a broken back. He built a Bible bookstore.

This is painful, so I understand if you prefer to keep this private. Please talk about Celeste, your sisterhood, and Celeste going home to be with our Lord...

How do I explain 60 years of friendship, arguing, getting mad at each other, and coming together for a cup of coffee without holding onto a grudge? We laughed together; we cried together; she had my back, and I had hers. How do I explain a closeness that is there every minute. She may have beat me to heaven...she left on December 11 at 2:32 PM...the electricity went out starting in her room and spread throughout the whole town of Soldotna. God told me audibly, so great a light has left the community. She cannot come to me, but one day

I will be able to go to her. A true friend sticks closer than a brother, I cannot express in words my relationship with Celeste. I do know she is sorely missed. I know I will see her again; she is in heaven where we all attain to reach one day, she completed her job. She did it well.

You have said, "Lord God, give them the revelation of who they are in You." What is the most important thing you would tell the new generation?

Trust the Word of God. Read it. Believe it, Stand in who you are in Christ, which takes us back to Mark 16... ALL who believe, this is ANYONE who calls on the name of the Lord. Trust Him; don't trust yourself.

The betrayal of false friends is so painful; we both know this well. You have described this pain as the wounds Jesus suffered that do not show. How do you cope with this pain?

Prayer, Forgiveness, Prayer, Forgiveness, more prayer, more forgiveness. It lifts, it goes away. God's love is greater. Imagine how Jesus suffered, yet He prayed, forgave, prayed, forgave. I am no better than my Master.

The times we are in are perilous. Any suggestion how to get through it?

My eyes can see, my ears can hear. Stupidity runs rampant. Nothing is the same as it used to be; things are perpetually changing for the worse. The Word of God never changes. It is a solid rock in my life; it should be a solid rock in everyone's life. You can trust God, you can trust Jesus, and you can trust the Holy Ghost. People will betray you. Jesus is the author and finisher, He called us, He chose us, He did a divine intervention so he could take what the world considers garbage and, if you truly trust him...well, then greater than I have done, you will do. Trust and believe in Christ and the Bible, not what you see or hear.

Regrets. Any?

No, not one. Bottom line is, we have to trust Him.

Chapter Twelve

Raising Up a
New Generation

Therefore, if anyone is in Christ, he is a new creation;
old things have passed away;
behold, all things have become new.

2 Corinthians 5:17

Forty years after Jesus appeared to her in the brothel, Vickie continues to call that small town in Alaska where God led her to while covered in His Glory, her home on earth.

Pastoring a congregation there, she calls the gathering place the "Ministry of the Living Stones." She says, "This is His Church"–not her church–HIS Church."

There, as she does all over the world, she teaches and preaches His Word unapologetically, with tremendous love and affection for every person who walks through the doors.

She knows God is making a way for each one of us when there isn't one. She teaches God is a respecter of no one, saying, "If He's done it for me, He will do it for you...if He does it for you, He will do it for me. Your job is to believe. Take your stand and walk in it."

Coming to Him as to a living stone,
rejected indeed by men,
but chosen by God and precious.
(1 Peter 2:4)

She emphasizes, "The Word of God is true, we are all liars, we need His Word in our Spirit!" Continuing, "The Old Testament tells us Who God is and what and why God does what He does; and the New Testament tells us how to live. If Jesus can do it, we can do it, too! He said so! You need to read the Bible!"

Vickie knows and teaches, "Anything you are going through, God is in the center of it. He said, 'I will never leave you nor forsake you' (Hebrews 13:5). And, Scripture says, 'If God is for us, who [and what] can be against us?' (Romans 8:31)."

"When you make a mistake, get up!" she preaches. "Stop beating yourself up. We are to be living epistles of His Word. Everything we say is being heard."

"When I was new in Christ, I had to have Him somewhere where I could reach Him, so I pretended He was in London. As I grew, I came to know I could go to His Throne—and so can you!" she says.

Vickie admits that she is easily influenced, and she says, "I am a weak woman. I can be led astray. I keep my circle small. I stay away from sin and remember that in my weakness, I find God in the center helping me."

"For the sake of Christ, then,
I am content with weaknesses,
insults, hardships, persecutions, and calamities.
For when I am weak, then I am strong"
2 Corinthians 12:10

She teaches, "We don't get to pick the ones to anoint, God does. Your walk is different than my walk, my walk is different than the person's over there. We are all called according to His purpose for us (Romans 8:28). The righteous are bold as lions; the wicked flee."

Every single thing that comes out of Vickie Walber's mouth is true to His Word, Spirit-led, for His Glory and our good.

God Almighty is in the center of these gatherings, I have not only witnessed miracles happen first hand in this blessed ministry, but I have also personally experienced a healing.

Vickie teaches us to grow in His Spirit according to His Word. She reminds us, "God said to the prophet Jeremiah, 'Before I formed you in the womb I knew you, before you were born I set you apart; I appointed you as a prophet to the nations.' Jeremiah answered, 'Alas, Sovereign LORD...I do not know how to speak; I am too young' (Jeremiah 1:5-6)."

"God knows our insecurities," she says. "There's a little bit of good in the worst of us, there's a little bit of bad in the rest of us. It does not behoove us to talk about the rest of us. If He can save *me*, he will save *you*, too. God makes a way when there isn't one (Isaiah 43:19)," she reminds us.

"God knows our insecurities. It's important to take responsibility for our actions," she tells us. "Our circumstances are of our own making. We live what we've created. God Himself will shake us up and reform us when we yield to Him. 'Now this, *Yet once more*, indicates the removal of those things that are being shaken, as of things that are made, that the things which cannot be shaken may remain' (Hebrews 12:27)."

Vickie reminds us that God knows what He's doing, and we cannot fathom His ways (Isaiah 55:8-9); we are called to obey Him in our insecurities.

She emphasizes, "Even Moses argued with God, revealing his self-doubt: 'Who am I that I should go?' he asked. And God responded, 'I will be with you. And…you will worship God on this mountain' (Exodus 3:11-12). 'What if they do not believe me or listen to me?' (Exodus 4:1). God proceeded to show Moses His Power and glory through miracles."

"Then Moses said to the Lord, 'O my Lord, I am not eloquent, neither before nor since You have spoken to Your servant; but I am slow of speech and slow of tongue.' So the Lord said to him, 'Who has made man's mouth? Or who makes the mute, the deaf, the seeing, or the blind? Have not I, the Lord? Now therefore, go, and I will be with your mouth and teach you what you shall say' (Exodus 4:10-12)."

~~~

Vickie encourages those whom she teaches. She knows Him. She loves Him.

She will say, "I am not telling you what to do, I am telling you what God expects from you. Get rid of the fear and pride that prevent you from using your gifts from Him.

"You are saved and sanctified! He saved my wretched soul. I was going to hell, just like you were going to hell. I was dead in sin. People who are dead don't know what they are doing. Don't think you are any better than the whore, the junkie, the alcoholic or anyone else dead in their sin, because you're not. You are saved by the same grace I am saved by and that mercy belongs to God.

"Memorizing the Bible will make you wise in your own eyes. We must live His Word. Love each other. Lift the alcoholic out of the gutter, not just pray he gets out himself. He can't. Our love requires action. Share what God has done for you! I'm just a dumb woman who used to be a hooker. He makes a way where there isn't one," she says.

"I need Jesus, and I need the Holy Spirit working in my life or I am not going to make it. Anything that separates us from God wants to kill us. Stop overthinking; ask the Holy Spirit! Matthew 7:21-23 tell us:

> *"Not everyone who says to Me, 'Lord, Lord,' shall enter the kingdom of heaven,*
> *but he who does the will of My Father in heaven.*
> *Many will say to Me in that day,*
> *'Lord, Lord, have we not prophesied in Your name,*
> *cast out demons in Your name, and done many wonders in Your name?'*
> *And then I will declare to them,*
> *'I never knew you; depart from Me, you who practice lawlessness!'"*

"How will He know who we are except for the love we have for each other? We do things out of love for each other. This is what God expects. This is what He commands of us."

~~~

Sierra

Vickie has taught me most of the things I know about Jesus Christ, and I have been forever changed because of how God has used her. One of the first and most important things she taught me about is the power of the Holy Spirit, that as a born-again Christian, the same

Spirit that breathed life into you, the same spirit that Jesus Christ performed miracles by, the same power that raised Jesus from the grave, dwells inside you, wants to use you, and is just waiting for you to yield yourself to him, you have the power and authority because of the Holy Spirit that dwells inside you. This revelation has changed my view not only of who God is, but who I am in him.

She also taught me about forgiveness, that it doesn't matter what someone did to you, made up lies, abused you, took advantage of your innocence, tried to kill you...if you don't forgive others, God won't forgive you. Forgiveness isn't for them, it's for you. When you forgive those who wronged you, it sets you free; free from anger, bitterness, torment, and hurt. It's not always something you can do in a day. It's something you choose to walk out every day. I choose to walk in forgiveness and put all those hurts in Jesus Christ's hands because it is what my Creator did for me and the standard He has called me to as His follower.

She always taught me to get a revelation for myself, to study a matter out, to not just believe anything you are fed by someone behind the pulpit or with a title. She taught me not to run to a commentary by man when you don't understand something but to get into your Bible and find a concept over and over again. She taught me that He is the same yesterday, today, and forever, and if it is of God, you will see it all throughout His word from Genesis to Revelation and when it's not something, just something you've been told, but something you have studied out and God himself has opened your eyes to, no one can take that from you.

She never wanted me dependent on her for answers but to always go to God for them. She often wouldn't give them to me when I asked but would always point me in the right direction of where I could start to find them. She wanted to make sure I could never be led astray by someone, because she taught me to never be dependent on man, but God and God alone.

Of the endless things this woman has taught me, I find these to be some of the most valuable lessons in my life.

Kalee

Vickie taught me to put my faith in God and not man, to rely on the Holy Spirit's voice instead of human words. This has rooted my faith in Jesus and given me a foundation to stand on. She taught me to study out a matter instead of hearing a message over a pulpit. That's the way the word becomes REAL to me.

She wouldn't just give me answers when I wanted them. She never made it too easy. She wanted me to think, to search, and to seek God for myself there are a lot of churches that don't do this with their people. As much as I loathed not having answers fed to me or immediate peace/satisfaction over a topic; I SO appreciate that she did this with me. It taught me to rely on the voice of the Holy Spirit, to get in my Bible and search for answers, and most importantly to have my own personal relationship with God. This was a fantastic way to teach patience in a generation that has everything at their fingertips.

She taught me how to love myself, to love who I am in Christ, and to fall in love with Jesus Christ in me. I had a terrible self-view because of my past that she showed me how to leave my sins in the sea of forgetfulness. God doesn't remember them. Why should I?! I am free in who God created me to be because of that woman.

She has taught me to stand when others came against me, to hold my tears when I wanted a pity party, to stand up and dust myself off and grab onto the hope that is Jesus. My security is in Jesus Christ. Not in who I was, or what I did. My life has transformed because of her guidance and counseling.

She pointed me in the right direction by using the Bible. She showed me what strength and dedication mean. She showed me what tenacity looks like. She taught me how to have a backbone and get things accomplished in the Kingdom, to have an undying relationship with the Lord Jesus.

And most importantly, that I can do all things through Christ who strengthens me (Philippians 4:13). I am more than a conqueror in Him, and I cannot fail.

Nicki

I've learned the meaning of integrity. Vickie was always doing what she said she was going to do and that fostered dependability in those who have not had a dependable person in their life. Keeping her word in the little things has garnered trust because if I could believe what she said about the little things, I could believe what she said about the things of Jesus Christ.

I've learned Christ-like behavior from Vickie. There's so much to say on this, but in a nutshell, Vickie lives what is talked about in the Bible with the choices she makes and with her actions. She doesn't talk about forgiveness she forgives the unforgivable. She doesn't talk about giving to the poor, or housing the homeless, or feeding the hungry, she actually does those things. Vickie is a living epistle, through her obedience and dedication to be uncomfortable in the pursuit of following the word of God to her own hurt.

This is not just something I have witnessed on occasion. A life of obedience is how this woman lives. Jesus is a lifestyle. The Holy Spirit is her friend, and I know God knows her by name. I have a living witness of humility and victory in Christ. I have gotten angry on her behalf because I only saw in the natural, when she sees past that into what she has placed at the forefront of her mind which is the word of God.

Vickie is always an advocate for the Church and for me. In regard to the church, Vickie hasn't given up on showing up. And she doesn't just show up, she hasn't abandoned her post as a caretaker of our souls, and I so respect her for that, having just the little knowledge I do of how messy and rotten and arduous the task of caring for a soul is.

In regard to me, Vickie defended me when I didn't expect it, before I had a voice to defend myself. In the little things, instances that seem insignificant, were significant to me, and the fact that she believed the Christ in me more than I believed was such a gift I didn't know I needed in my early walk.

Jeana

Vickie taught me to always keep my lamp full. Always be ready because you never know when you will be called. Keep reading the word, praying, praising, and worshipping the lord. You always have to be ready in season and out of season.

She's taught me not to put myself in a box or put limits or mental restrictions on myself. She said, "Don't think, 'Oh, it's just a prayer.' Prayer is powerful! Jesus intercedes for us!"

If we are an open yielded vessel to the Lord Jesus, He will use us for His glory. She taught me to keep my eyes on the Lord Jesus. She would tell me, "Keep your hands to the plow and don't look back. Always keep moving forward."

Vickie taught me, "Don't seek man's approval, seek God's." Turn to the Bible and turn to God for learning and wisdom. Ask God to lead you and direct you. Seek Him first in all you do. Don't be afraid of what people will say or think of you.

"Be bold as a lion, gentle as a dove."

She also taught me the only thing that matters is what God thinks.

Janine

Seeking man's approval is a surefire way of being disappointed in yourself, and you'll never be satisfied. It is a no-win game. Seek your approval from God. Find out what he wants and do it. Spending time with God is key. Separate yourself from the trappings of the world and the business of your soul and dive into his grace and his mercy and seek to understand who he is and who you are in him.

Forgiveness is an action that is not for the person who did the hurting, but it is for you to heal and move on. Forgiveness is a release, a shedding off, and is the first part of truly healing.

Dominique

Vickie has taught me the way you live your life is a direct reflection of your heart condition and your love for Jesus Christ. I learned this strictly by watching Vickie's life for the last 25 years. Everywhere she goes and anyone she comes into contact with, to the best of her ability, she tries to share her knowledge of Jesus Christ because she knows He is the one who saves. Vickie has experienced His goodness, salvation, love, grace, mercy, and faithfulness, and doesn't wish anyone to miss the opportunity of knowing Him. Her life and leadership remind me of this scripture: "Imitate me, just as I also imitate Christ" (1 Corinthians 11:1).

While we were on a mission trip, I was able to have a lot of personal conversations with Vickie. At this time in my life, I had the hardest time accepting the fact that God would and/or wanted to use me for any purpose in his Kingdom. I would unknowingly drag old shame back into my life. I walked around carrying so much weight on my shoulders from things I had already repented for. I had this, "Why me?" mindset, thinking I was unworthy of a calling from the Lord. I constantly disqualified myself for use. Vickie pulled me aside and simply stated, "Why NOT you?" She spoke to me about false humility. You see, it was at this moment, I realized that the person I kept dragging around was someone who died the moment I accepted Jesus Christ as my Lord and Savior. I was a new creation, with a new spiritual family, calling, purpose, and a clean slate. If Jesus said I was able, worthy, and fit to be used in his Kingdom, who am I to tell Him He is wrong? I had been walking in false humility (which is still pride) by keeping the "Why me?" mindset.

Something I've had the privilege of learning from Vickie, by not only watching her life, but by her pushing me in my own faith in how to truly trust the Holy Spirit. The Holy Spirit was sent to be with us when Jesus ascended. He is meant to be our closest friend, mentor, guide, comforter, and teacher, and is our source of power. There are things that we may be called or asked to do by the Holy Spirit that do not make any logical sense, but when you do it, you see it work out better than you could have imagined. There have been circumstances in my life that have forced me to lean on the Holy Spirit for help, and every single time, he has been faithful to show up.

Vickie lives her life in constant fellowship with the Holy Spirit, and you see the fruit of that relationship work in every aspect of her life. Her life is an inspiration, and motivation to any Spirit-filled believer.

Chapter Thirteen

Faith

*Now faith is the substance of things hoped for,
the evidence of things not seen.*

Hebrews 11:1

"We all start somewhere," Vickie preaches, "I am a valued vessel of God since the day I walked out of the whorehouse. God will operate in your life if you let Him. 'The kingdom of heaven is like a mustard seed, which a man took and sowed in his field, which indeed is the least of all the seeds; but when it is grown it is greater than the herbs and becomes a tree, so that the birds of the air come and nest in its branches'" (Matthew 13:31-32).

"I play by the rules in the House of the Lord," she explains. "I trust in God. The Lord Jesus is first in my life, and He needs to be first in your life.

"Have faith!" Vickie says, "Religion will not save you. Only God can save you, and no one gets to the Father except through the Son, Jesus! (John 14:6)

And since we have the same spirit of faith, according to what is written,
"I believed and therefore I spoke,"
we also believe and therefore speak,
knowing that He who raised up the Lord Jesus
will also raise us up with Jesus and will present us with you.
For all things are for your sakes, that grace, having spread through the many,
may cause thanksgiving to abound to the glory of God.
Therefore, we do not lose heart.

Even though our outward man is perishing,
yet the inward man is being renewed day by day.
For our light affliction, which is but for a moment,
is working for us a far more exceeding and eternal weight of glory,

while we do not look at the things which are seen, but at the things which are not seen.

For the things which are seen are temporary, but the things which are not seen are eternal.

2 Corinthians 4:13-18

Walking in Faith and Trusting Him, He Shows Us the Way

Kalee

There is power in the name of Jesus, not my own, His. I didn't know the fullness of the name of Jesus until this trip to the Philippines. I didn't have to touch people; I didn't have to say a special prayer. All I needed was the indwelling of the Holy Spirit. The Holy Spirit upon us all; the name of Jesus is everything. People were getting delivered, healed, and set free.

I had no time to prepare. No time to study at night. No time to breathe or think. I wanted to write a thought-out, well-planned sermon, and I never got the chance. This showed me that I have a never-ending wellspring of His Holy Spirit living inside of me. I had all I had needed with Him when ministering to the people, when praying with the people. We were ready. I got to see the fivefold ministry in action. I got to see how a group works together, how Spirit-led gifting complements each other and the strength each gift brings to the group.

The Bible says disciples were sent out in twos. We had a dynamic team, and I got to see everyone operating in their giftings from the Holy Spirit. I got to see how God's grace, poured out on each one of us, fluently operates in a team. I got to see love within the body of Jesus Christ, God's love for the lost, and the love God has for His servants. No one was in competition with each other. We were a unit.

I got set free as well as the people. When you allow God to come in and pull out things hidden deep within you, you can receive a healing. I got to open up and let parts of myself go that I was holding on to. God revealed things to me that I wasn't able to see before.

Forgiveness was the biggest one. Forgive and be set free so you can be used mightily in the Kingdom!

I can do all things through Jesus Christ. I didn't have full revelation of this scripture before this trip.

I looked at myself as common or unable to do the job. I tell you that ANYTHING is possible when your faith is in Him. I felt like I was going along for a ride, but the Holy Spirit was operating through me and using my hands. God used my hands to cast out demons and heal broken lives. I didn't have to do anything. He did it, I just had to be yielded and willing. Yield yourself to the Lord God, that's what He wants.

God was moving powerfully. God has a plan for that nation, and He used us to do it. It was the most humbling experience of my life. It will never be the same. I am thankful for our leadership, for Vickie, and for the work God is doing in the hearts of the people there.

Sierra

When we got to the Philippines we hit the ground running. There was no time to read our Bibles, no time to prepare a sermon, no time to go over the notes and sermons we had already prepared prior to the trip. There was one day we did six services. Six in one day, back-to-back! There was no time to think or breathe in between. It felt stressful for a moment but I am so thankful for the experience. It taught me to trust the Word that has been placed inside me on a level that I hadn't had to do before.

We had no choice but to follow the leading of the Holy Spirit. We didn't know if we were being asked to sing, give a testimony, or preach a Word. We didn't even know what subject they would be leading the service with until we started. We never had our notes or Bibles in our hand when we would walk up. It was just you and whatever God wanted to pour through you in that moment, and boy did He pour it out.

When we went to pray for people, the altar was so full every time. People collapsed under the power of God the moment we would touch them or breathe on them. We had Words for people, they were healed, set free, it was amazing. I knew God could do those things. I've seen Him do those things. I didn't doubt that, but to have Him use my hands, to pour His Spirit out through me, on that magnitude, I have a new level of assurance of what He has given to me and what He wants all his people to walk in.

It was one of the most glorious times in Jesus Christ in my entire life.

I got to see the stark contrast of another pastor we were ministering with that had come with everything he had prepared, and one of the days the Spirit was ministering to him, he got up to start his portion of the session and said, "I am going to get out of the way of what the Spirit wants to do before I get to what I have prepared for you." The words disturbed me. We can be so focused on what we have prepared, what our agenda is, or how we think it should go, that we completely miss what the Spirit of the Lord God wants to do.

If he had pressed into that Word that God had given him, it could have been Holy Spirit fire! Instead, he gave a Word from the Lord and then cut that power by continuing with what he wanted to do. Don't doubt what you know, and don't get pulled into their religious garbage.

People will try to compete with you, but they can't compete with God. It should always be God working inside each of us as we minister together, pulling out a different piece and using a different gifting in each of us. Our team came together in an incredible way. There was no competition amongst us, no feelings of inferiority, just the same Holy Spirit working through each of us in a different way.

I got to see the fivefold ministry (Ephesians 4:11-13) in action on the mission field. When we were ministering at the conference there were many different denominations and people with different theologies that had come together. They didn't always appear to listen to what others had to say depending on who was speaking, but one thing I watched them all come together in was praise and worship. One thing that we can always unify on is praise of our great God. It is powerful and breaks down the walls that sometimes divides us as Christians.

One of the days we were there, there was a person ministering to the people who was talking about overcoming failure. The conference was on "The Overcomer." The topic didn't sit well with me. The word failure really isn't in the Bible, it only occurs in three scriptures and none of them are talking about us. We often feel like we have failed in parts of our lives, but that's not something God ever calls us. "Failure" is a label we put on ourselves and each other, it is not biblical. God calls us overcomers. You don't fail. You sin. We are called to repent of our sins, get up, and do better.

Jeana

The presence of God was overwhelming as we sat there in the presence of His people who were genuinely worshipping and praising Him. You could feel His overwhelming presence in that place. You could see the pure joy, love, and adoration on their faces as they sang to Him, danced, and prayed.

We prayed with and for people not just once, but some days multiple times in that day. The number of people who came up to pray was incredible. So many people were moved by the power of God. The Spirit of the Lord God moved freely.

We went there thinking we would be a blessing to the people in the Philippines, and it turned out they were a blessing to us and to me.

They have nothing compared to the lavish things we have here in the United States. We have houses that may be small to us but are large to them, a vehicle or some of us even have two, we have toilet paper, we have water to wash our hands. We have so much compared to them yet what we have are material treasures here on earth.

In the Philippines, God is their All, their Everything.

On Sunday, there were three services, the first one started at 6:00 AM, ending at noon. As each one of the services ended and the next one started, the presence of the Lord God was stronger than the previous one. The praise and worship were stronger, you could see how those around us were affected by His presence. It was beautiful and humbling to see how openly the Lord God was worshipped without shame or worry about what someone else would think of them. I am certain God said, "These are my people."

I learned not to let my guard down; we need to stay ready and take charge when the enemy attacks. Pray over yourself in your spiritual language of tongues and take authority. Be alert. The enemy attacked on the way to South Korea. I let my guard down after we left the Philippines and was not prepared, nor did I take charge over the situation. Now, I know better.

Janine

The Bible says through our weaknesses we are made strong (2 Corinthians 12:9-10). When we make a mistake and follow the wrong path, as soon as we realize it, we need to repent, and we need to move forward. God will continue to meet us and forgive us when we come to Him asking for forgiveness. We must repent, which means we acknowledge the wrong, and turn away from it. It comes down to yielding to God's will and not our will.

The anointing of God makes a deposit that we can draw upon. Through true worship and yielding, we can call upon Him. He is present in the true praise of His people, and He will be present where they call out to him. We all have the opportunity to receive and walk in the anointing of God. We need to be yielded to Him.

Nicki

I learned the power of personal testimony in the Philippines. Prior to this trip, I had not fully understood the extent of how powerful one's personal testimony is, the capacity it has for true freedom and healing. I saw those giving testimonies become freer each time they spoke. I watched those around them identify and be encouraged by the testimonies of the peace, freedom, and healing that Jesus Christ offers, replacing shame, guilt, and victimhood.

Those testimonies were witnesses of the ability to overcome through Jesus Christ, and a door to salvation open for those who were able to seek God's glory; lives of people who should, in the natural, be broken by their experiences. I witnessed living examples of how repentance and choosing Jesus Christ replaces sin and death with a life worth living.

The joy and happiness that the Philippine people have for Jesus Christ is genuine, and the freedom to worship freely and with an open heart is not something that is commonly seen in the United States. The freedom to worship is an invitation for the Holy Spirit to freely move amongst His people. Those in attendance at the services were ready to receive and that stemmed largely from the relationship they had established with God and the priority He has in their lives. This contrasted so sharply with the typical compartmentalization and shallow segregation between "church life" and a "worldly lifestyle" so common in the United States.

The power of the Holy Spirit manifesting in the team that went was unexpected in that each person who went was used. I truly saw that God is no respecter of persons, if the servant was willing, that vessel was used for His glory!

Understanding that the authority that we carry, given to us by Jesus Christ, is precious and healing and powerful. Witnessing that authority cast out demons and speak life over the broken and dead in sin, completely disregarded the natural in that it's not what I can do, or what I think, or even what I feel. It's what God says, and it's who Jesus Christ is.

The ways that God demonstrated Himself through the various moves of the Holy Spirit was so varied it was quite interesting and surprisingly unexpected.

Dominique

There is power in your testimony. When you share your testimony, you are telling the saving power of Jesus Christ. You should never compare your testimony to other people's testimonies or doubt the impact your testimony can make. Your testimony is not about you, or where you came from. It is about the transformation that Jesus has done in your life. When you talk about the power and glory of the Lord Jesus Christ, the Holy Spirit is at work to plant seeds in the hearts of those who need to know Him. Your testimony encourages faith.

The Kingdom of God is not a one man show. There is no competition in ministry. We are not to be working alone. God will place people in your life to help your ministry and use you to help theirs, all for the glory of God. I watched and experienced the fivefold ministry (Ephesians 4:11-13) in action, and it was dynamic.

God will use you when you are willing and yielded. It doesn't matter who you are, things you've done, or what you think of yourself. If you make yourself available to Him, He will move dramatically through you. When you take yourself out of the equation and trust the Holy Spirit, He will work through you as a vessel for His glory.

I now realize how "religion" binds you up. Before we left for the Philippines, I was studying the Word for hours daily, praying, fasting, seeking the Lord God, trying to prepare for the work He wanted us to accomplish. I was trying to have everything laid out. I wanted God to give me all the sermons beforehand, I was expecting to know the itinerary. I wanted to be prepared. But, I've come to know, in this mindset, you push away the Holy Spirit.

Yes, in general, you should pray, read, fast, to draw nearer to the Lord God. This was not my reason for doing these things, I just wanted the itinerary. I wanted it to be prepared as if it was for work. God did not give me any sermons! It was a very quiet two weeks before our trip! I was forced to rely on faith, and now, I praise the Lord God for this lesson! I didn't understand at the time that my motivation was trying to put God in a box somehow.

We were so busy going from service to service as soon as we arrived in the Philippines. We would wake up at 5:00 AM and go to sleep at midnight daily for two weeks. One day we did six services. I spoke at just about every single one. The only thing I was asked to speak on was my testimony. I only had time to read my Bible twice the entire trip. Even though I wasn't prepared in my way of thinking, I realize now that the Holy Spirit is all I needed! I didn't need notes or prepared sermons, I needed Him! The Holy Spirit is the One who draws people near, changes hearts, plants the Word. He is our only source of power. I am the vessel.

"Religion" binds, His Holy Spirit frees!

As civilized as Americans like to think they are, we really live in our own little bubble here. There are so many people in the world who are desperate to know the Lord God. People, like the ones we met in the Philippines, those who have nothing, know Jesus is all they need. When they don't have access to a doctor, they go to Jesus for healing and receive it because of their faith! The time they are given in a day is dedicated to the Lord God because of all He provides for them.

Americans could learn from the people in the Philippines. Here, we have everything we could ever want or need, and because of this so many forget that ALL things come from God. The job you have, the money you make, your health, your family, everything, all is granted by God Himself. God deserves all glory and credit in every aspect of your life. God is your source. He alone deserves the glory and praise. We must stop our dependence on everything else.

Chapter Fourteen

Serving

He who dwells in the secret place of the Most High
Shall abide under the shadow of the Almighty.
I will say of the Lord, "He is my refuge and my fortress;
My God, in Him I will trust."

Psalm 91:1-2

The precious gift of the Holy Spirit has miraculously led, taught, and blessed Vickie and those who God brought to her who needed His help. She says, "I have seen tens of thousands of people transformed from drugs, child abuse, and dysfunctional lives. Marriages have been restored. All glory to God!"

Vickie's mission continues to this day, to counsel the hurting, the broken, and the downtrodden; to see men, women, and children made healthy and whole in Jesus Christ, spiritually, mentally, and physically.

There are thousands of documented healings and miracles through the powerful anointing granted to her by the Glory of God, including raising people from the dead, witnessing people healed of physical ailments including hepatitis C, HIV, broken backs, broken bones, diabetes, cold and flu illnesses, cancers, and infertility.

Vickie has witnessed—firsthand—God healing broken hearts and broken minds, and has witnessed emotional stresses healed through wisdom, compassion, and love, through the power of His Holy Spirit.

She has helped numerous people to get out of the national welfare system, watched as God healed drug addicts, criminals, and alcoholics from every walk of life. She has witnessed them being restored and reconciled back to God. They and their families have become valid, viable citizens in their communities. "God is so very merciful. His grace is forever abounding" she says.

Vickie has organized charity auctions for the rehabilitation of prisoners seeking a new way of life. She has organized charity auctions to provide education and personal counseling for troubled youth, preventing them from having a ruined life of criminal activity.

She founded the Academy of Higher Learning, a Christian School recognized by the State of Alaska. There, students are able to grow in Christian character and develop academically without fear of personal safety.

Vickie started a youth ministry at the Academy called, "The International Mime" team, and provided vocational training in the housing construction trade, including home building and home remodeling, carpentry, cooking, computers, and childcare—all as an outreach ministry for youth at risk.

She has provided Christian housing for the underprivileged. In addition to personally housing those at risk, she has counseled and pastored many people into leading productive, holy lives.

Miraculous Accomplishments:

1983 Instituted the first Foursquare Church in Soldotna, Alaska

1984 Started the Ministry of the Living Stones

1992 Started the second Ministry of the Living Stones in Anchorage, Alaska

1994 Built the Academy of Higher Learning for K-12 in Sterling, Alaska

1997 Established the Ministry of the Living Stones Bible Institute of Alaska

2005 Guest Speaker at the Alaska Governor's Prayer Breakfast in Juneau, Alaska

2007 Built Studio G, a catalyst for Alaska's rural youth into the media industry

2007 Biography, *Angel of the Flesh*, published

2009 Filmed *48 Below*, written by Verissa Walber and Tina Wegener, and featuring local Alaskan youth

2011 Winner of the "Spirit Award" at the International Family Film Festival for *48 Below*

2011 Received ownership rights to the film, *The 5th Floor*, released in the early 1970s

2014 Speaker and Host for the Conference "Kingdom Big – Infusion of Power"

2014 Speaker and Host for the Conference "Double Portion Conference"

2014 Speaker and Host for the Conference "Missionary to the Nations"

2018 Host for "Praise and Worship," Guest Speaker, Apostle Deborah Fraser, in Sterling, Alaska

2023 Ministry of the Living Stones 62-day Repentance and Revival Conference, "Raising Up Millennials Into Gifting and Calling"

National Ministry:

1986   Started the Freedom Center in Washington, DC

1995 - Present Guest Speaker in Washington, Oregon, California, Wisconsin, Oklahoma, Texas, and Virginia

2003 - 2004   Received a letter and phone calls from the White House and Senate affirming Ministry and works

2005   Invited to participate in Presidential Prayer Breakfast in Washington, DC

2006   Invited to participate in Presidential Prayer Breakfast in Washington, DC

2007   Correspondence with Ambassador Tony Hall's representatives

2007   Correspondence with Evangelical Doug Coe

2007   Worked closely with Christian media leaders nationally

2007   Invited to be Guest Speaker at North Carolina and Oklahoma evangelical events

2013   Guest Speaker and Advisor for the 40-Day Awakening Event in Kenai, Alaska

International Ministry:

1985 Conference Speaker in the Philippines; healed by God of cholera while speaking to pastoral attendees. Guest Speaker in various Philippine villages, Holy Spirit yielded performing miraculous healings and thousands led to salvation as a yielded vessel of His Holy Spirit

1985 - Present
      Met with Heads of State, Presidents, Royalty, and Tribal Chieftains around the world often with an invitation to return any time

1994 Built a retreat center in Naranjo, Costa Rica
1994 Worked hand in hand with other ministries in Central
      and South America; received an open invitation from Cuba
      to return.
1994 Evangelized in Central and South America
1994 Conference Speaker for Vineyard Ministries in San Jose,
      Escazu, Costa Rica
1995 Distributed 10,000 Bibles in Costa Rica
1995 Invited to the palace to visit the First Lady of Costa Rica
1995 Trunks of school supplies were delivered to the teachers
      of Costa Rica; worked closely with other international
      ministries at the Teachers Conference in Costa Rica's "Touch
      a Child, Change a Nation" Ministry while the teachers were
      on strike in Costa Rica
1995 Ministry trip to Peru
1995 Distributed 55,000 Bibles in Peru
1995 Sponsored, trained, and ministered with the International
      Mime Team from Alaska in the schools of Lima, Peru
1995 Three ministry trips to Nicaragua
1996 Worked closely with other international ministries to bring
      running water, electricity and industry to El Comejen,
      Nicaragua. We personally provided finances, tools, four
      sewing machines, fabrics, and trunks of school supplies to
      the village in an effort to help the people there to become
      self-sufficient.
1996 Sponsored the International Mime Team in churches and
      orphanages in and around Managua, Nicaragua
1996 Delivered trunks of medical supplies to the hospitals
      and community medical centers in Managua, Nicaragua
1996 Assisted in opening the only Christian radio station in
      Nicaragua
1996 Guest Speaker on TBN several times, 700 club, and the
      only Christian radio station in Nicaragua. Program tapes
      were taken to Mexico, resulting in miraculous healings there.

1996   Guest Speaker in Mexico

1997   Provided monthly support for soup kitchens to continue and increase in number in Managua, Nicaragua

1997   Ministered at the National Pastor's convention in Managua, Nicaragua where there were 2,500 pastors present

1998   Conference Speaker in Panama

1998   Keynote Speaker at a Pastoral Conference in Costa Rica

1998   Speaker at the College of the Desert in Palm Springs

1998   Raised tens of thousands of dollars for Nicaraguan victims of Hurricane Mitch, the ministry fed hundreds of children, three times a week, through a feeding program we set up in Managua, Nicaragua

1998   Set up a camp for thousands of displaced families in Nicaragua

2000 - 2001
        Ministered in Brazil

2000   Taught English to the locals in Brazil

2005   Pastoral conferences in Africa

2006   Attended national leadership conferences in Africa

2006   Started feeding programs for thousands of children and adults, building programs and training centers in Africa

2007   Israeli ministry trip; was invited to open church by local community leaders in Bethlehem

2008   Served in Uganda, Africa, at a children's orphanage and helped start a youth ministry

2012   Kenya, Africa, opened a training center for missionaries, built orphanages, feeding centers, and a senior women's center

2017   Was a Host and Guide for "Footsteps of Jesus" in Israel and Jordan

2018   Ministry of the Living Stones, Speaker, at the international leadership conference in Nairobi, Kenya, in Africa

2019   International Ministries of the Living Stones, foundational teacher; feeding program implemented in Nazas, Durango, in Mexico

2020   International Ministries of the Living Stones, foundational
       teacher, feeding program, establishing mission
2021   International Ministries of the Living Stones, foundational
       teacher, feeding program, building industry, praying over the
       land for a church building
2022   International Ministries of the Living Stones, foundational
       teacher, continuing to establish mission
2023   Speaker, International Leader Conference in Nairobi, Kenya,
       Africa

~~~

Vickie Walber's educational credentials are sturdy–remember,
Vickie could not read or write until the blessed appearance of our
Lord and Savior Jesus changed everything that day in the brothel!

1983 – Present
Instruction and Inspiration by the Holy Spirit

Passed GED Exam

1985
The United Church and Ministerial Association
Biblical Associate

1987 Calvary Theological Seminary
Bachelor of Arts, Christian Counseling, earning a GPA 4.0

1988
Ordination in the New Covenant Christian Church

1998
The National Christian Counselors Association
Certification in Biblical Counseling

1999 Participation in Master's degree studies
Pastoral Counseling
Substance Abuse Counseling
Addiction Counseling
Crisis and Abuse Counseling
Suicide/Teen Suicide Counseling

2003 Certified Clergy Authorization
Prison Ministry/Alaska Correctional Facilities

~~~

"Jesus is interceding for me," Vickie says.

One of Vickie's most personally quoted verses from the Bible is this:

What then shall we say to these things?
If God is for us, who can be against us?
He who did not spare His own Son, but delivered Him up for us all,
how shall He not with Him also freely give us all things?
Who shall bring a charge against God's elect? It is God who justifies.
Who is he who condemns?
It is Christ who died, and furthermore is also risen, who is even at
the right hand of God, who also makes intercession for us. Who shall
separate us from the love of Christ? Shall tribulation, or distress,
or persecution, or famine, or nakedness, or peril, or sword? As it is
written:
"For Your sake we are killed all day long;
We are accounted as sheep for the slaughter."
Yet in all these things we are more than conquerors through Him who
loved us.
For I am persuaded that neither death nor life, nor angels nor
principalities nor powers,

nor things present nor things to come, nor height nor depth, nor any other created thing,

shall be able to separate us from the love of God which is in Christ Jesus our Lord.

Romans 8:31-39

Close to forty years ago, Vickie and her husband David met a man named Winston when they were all at a conference together in Oklahoma. This is what Pastor Winston has to say about his ministry with Vickie:

> Pastor Vickie and I have known each other for many years. We met briefly at a conference in Oklahoma, then never spoke to each other for a while. However, she searched me out, I had gone through a test and trial, the Lord sent her to my life to minister to my Spirit.

> I went to Alaska upon her invitation, she had words of wisdom, exhortation and encouragement for myself to go out and do the work the Lord desired for me. I have since evangelized the world.

> Pastor Vickie is a friend, mentor, and confidant. We have ministered together across the nations. Ministry of the Living Stones has faithfully supported my ministry since the beginning. They helped to purchase, physically build, and preach in the Mission Center built in Nairobi, Kenya.

> My son was gravely ill, Vickie called to pray for him. I knew without any doubt that if my son did not recover it was because the Lord himself was taking him home. She prayed with the authority that I have seen heal people of disease, be released from demonic oppression, however my son wasn't healed. My heart is at rest because it was his time to go to be with our Savior.

> I have seen snow at the equator in Kenya, after Pastor Vickie prayed for an answer regarding personal questions.

I have the upmost respect for her as a sister in Christ, as a leader, and as a confidant.   ~ Pastor Winston

~~~

God loves us all so very much. Vickie reminds us, "He saved me from myself—and He can save you, too. Invite Him into your life. It's that simple. He's waiting for you. When you experience His love and mercy, you will want to change anything in yourself that would possibly offend Him. Jesus tells us, *'Peace I leave with you, My peace I give to you; not as the world gives do I give to you. Let not your heart be troubled, neither let it be afraid'* (John 14:27)."

"Saved, you will want to help other people, to love them into His Kingdom just as you and I are loved by Him," she says. "Go and be baptized in water, be baptized in His Holy Spirit. When Jesus was baptized in water in the River Jordan, He stood up and a dove appeared over His head — He received the Power of His Holy Spirit at that moment to begin His ministry on earth. That same Holy Spirit Power from God is available to you! He loves us that much!"

After His death and Resurrection, before He ascended into heaven, Jesus told us He would send His Holy Spirit to be with us always,

And I will pray the Father, and He will give you another Helper,
that He may abide with you forever—
the Spirit of truth, whom the world cannot receive,
because it neither sees Him nor knows Him;
but you know Him, for He dwells with you and will be in you.
I will not leave you orphans; I will come to you.
"A little while longer and the world will see Me no more, but you will
see Me.
Because I live, you will live also.
At that day you will know that I am in My Father,
and you in Me, and I in you.
John 14:16-20

"Jesus is handing you the keys to His Kingdom—you don't have to go through another human person, priest, pope, rabbi, or some-such to get them—He is handing them directly to you. Go and be baptized in His Holy Spirit and let Him work through you, too. *Most assuredly, I say to you, unless one is born of water and the Spirit, he cannot enter the kingdom of God'* (John 3:5)."

"Baptized in His Holy Spirit, your anointing will not be the same as mine, mine will not be the same as yours, nor should it be. With Him, we can do miraculous things, without Him, we cannot accomplish one thing. He will use you according to His ways, for His Glory and our good (Romans 8:28)," Vickie says.

"Remember, our circumstances are of our own making. 'Seek ye the Kingdom of God first' (Matthew 6:33). God always makes a way when there isn't one. With Him, we can do miraculous things, without Him, we cannot accomplish one worthwhile thing," Vickie teaches.

Vickie encourages us, "Let Him use you! Let Him work through you! Be His vessel for His Glory and your good! Praise Him in all things—both good and challenging. He is with us!"

These things I have spoken to you,
that in Me you may have peace.
In the world you will have tribulation;
but be of good cheer, I have overcome the world.

John 16:33

Part Two

What Do They Say?

Testimonies of Faith, Healing, and Deliverance

Blessed are your eyes for they see, and your ears for they hear.

Matthew 13:16

Tina

God has given me a unique blessing in life. I have been Verissa "Vickie" Walber's assistant for twenty-two years, and a member of Ministry of the Living Stones for an additional four years. I have lived with Vickie and David for almost 15 years. I have travelled to many nations with Vickie.

Describing Vickie, one could use words such as authoritative, bold, compassionate, loyal, loving, integrity, apostolic, educator, healer, servant, pastoral, and handmaiden. Handmaiden is how she prefers to be called when people want to put a title next to her name. Titles are of no importance to Vickie, salvation and the Cross are the factors in life that lead her life.

I can attest and confirm most of the miracles that many people may speak about, because I was in the room with Vickie. I have witnessed a woman raised from the dead. I have seen possessed people for years set free, bodies healed.

Examples of healings would include broken bones miraculously healed, broken backs mended, muscles and tendons sewn together, and hearts with physical holes repaired, to but name a few. People, men, women and children set free from the spirit of oppression, the spirit of jealousy, legions, which led to more complete lives for them and their walks with Jesus Christ.

I, myself, have had numerable physical healings. My back was healed after a commercial-sized cappuccino machine fell on it, broken bones, and sprained muscles. However, that is the least that I have seen in my life.

The greatest miracle was the gift of Salvation. I know that this is the greatest miracle in a person's life for a person was once dead, with no hope, and is now alive in Jesus Christ. Vickie has led thousands, hundreds of thousands to Jesus Christ, in stadiums, to a restaurant bathroom, where one receives Salvation doesn't matter. Across the globe Vickie will speak the name of Jesus, a dirt road, a bus, a highway, a limousine, it doesn't matter to her—everyone is equal in the eyes of God. She walks this, she speaks this, and she shares this compassion with whomever will listen or at the very least be in hearing distance.

Vickie is my friend, my spiritual leader, my spiritual mother, but even more so she is my sister in Jesus Christ. She has been through every unthinkable issue in life with me, beside me, praying for me, with me, shedding tears, fighting in Jesus Christ's authority.

These few words do not encapsulate everything, I could write or speak. This I know, "It is a great life, if you don't weaken…" and that I have learned along with so much more from Verissa Walber.

Thankfulness isn't a strong enough word—Glory to God!

Anonymous

I met Vickie Walber in 1990, under what seemed like normal circumstances to me. I am a hairdresser, and she came to get her hair done. She kept coming and coming, to the point where her hair couldn't take one more anything, if she wanted any hair on her head. She was persistent.

These circumstances were anything but normal. Her mission from God was to introduce me to the Jesus that she knew. The Jesus that works just like He did in the New Testament. The One that takes broken lives and rebuilds them.

I knew of Jesus and went to church many years before. However, my encounter with Vickie, well, from that day forward my life has gone from a state of brokenness, despair, and desperation, to one of strength, stability, and confidence. I could do all things through Jesus. She knows. She assured me.

It began that day in the beauty shop where I worked. Only God knows the depth of where and how that friendship in Him would go. All that time, my life was broken in every way you could imagine. My husband was in and out of prison, violent, into drugs and women, and even tried to kill me.

I worked two jobs while going to college and put up a good front. I could pretend with the best of them. God knowing, He used his faithful and obedient servant to show me the way to Him. She encouraged me over and over and pointed me to Jesus and His words. I am truly not that same person that would avoid people and did not want to be seen or heard. It was an existence, not life.

I can thank God for using her to show me the way to having real life in Jesus Christ and for my rebuilt life.

The dead have risen, the rain comes in the days of drought, demons flee, sickness and disease gone, people healed. I have witnessed miracles done through Vickie and because she believed Jesus could, others benefited.

Truly, Vickie is an inspiration of who Jesus Christ is, and what He will do through a willing vessel. She is the first to tell you, "I am not special, just willing and obedient." We have walked together in Jesus Christ all these years. I have seen God use her to rebuild lives everywhere she goes, that truly is one of the greatest things to watch. Hope being restored.

She is determined and persistent to be used by God for His glory. I have seen her walk in the power of Jesus, showing that Jesus is alive today, and He is using faithful obedient servants just as herself.

Thank You Jesus for saving this one, and for the masses to see Your Glory!

Jeana

Vickie's leadership in the church is profound, the message she speaks always lines up with the Word of God, and she tirelessly proclaims His Word to us, the congregation, so that we may be saved, snatching us from our own detriment. Vickie is kind and loving, she has the patience to give us guidance and direction, helps us when we are stuck in the Word, and is always leading and aligning with the Word of God.

I met Vickie through my sister about eight years ago and have been part of Ministry of the Living Stones for almost four years. I have learned so much from Vickie. With my own eyes, I have seen Vickie pray over people and see them set free from demons, I've seen people healed from sickness, and I've heard the angels in heaven sing with us as we sang praises and worshiped at MLS.

Vickie never stops telling people about the goodness of Jesus, how He saved her and what He has done in her life. I have learned and am still learning from Vickie to be bold in Jesus Christ; it doesn't matter what other people, or the world think of you, it matters what God thinks of you.

You know when Vickie has arrived without even having to look around, you can feel God with her as she enters the building. One time, I was up at the front of the church praying while the praise team was singing, and I knew Vickie had arrived. The only way I can compare it to was like the burning bush with Moses. I didn't even need to turn around to know she was there.

Hearing Vickie sing makes me cry. I can hear how much she loves her Father in heaven, singing to Him with all her heart and might. I can hear her devotion to Him. It's beautiful.

Last year, I broke my foot on a Saturday while in California, and as we praised, prayed, and sang the next day (via YouTube), God healed my foot. God has healed my heart and given me the gift of peace, things I never even knew were possible.

I thank God for Vickie and for MLS. The Lord God almighty is there, He is there walking amongst us, expectantly waiting for us to come to Him.

Mary

Tuesday, August 20th, 2024, my Uncle John called me. He said, "Hey, Mary, do you have a second to talk?" After answering his question, he went on to say that he was blown away at being at our house for the week and enjoyed learning about my husband Vince and me.

He said, "I've spent years being angry at God only to find out that it wasn't God I was mad at, but 'religion.'" He thanked me again for bringing him to my church and told me he was looking forward to coming back.

Two days earlier, on August the 18th, we stood as a church together and prayed for two people, one of those persons was my Uncle Mike, the shorter of the two men who were sitting in the back pew.

I sent him a text message on Monday, August the 19th, asking for forgiveness, because I hadn't prayed for him while he was visiting us. I told him that as Christians we are called to lay hands on the sick and claim healing over their bodies, but Vince and I failed in doing that while he was at our house.

Anyway, I explained that my Church prayed for him for complete healing over his body. Then I said, "Uncle, you stated that you have been praying for healing and because it hadn't happened you believed that it wasn't going to ever happen."

So, I explained to him that when you pray and ask for anything, but put a time limit on it, you are really the one working for the miracle and not allowing God. "However, if you really believe in God's healing, I want you to believe that your healing came last Sunday. Do you believe?" He replied, "Yes!"

On Wednesday, August 21st, my uncle called me to let me know that it was the first time in 45 years that he woke up without pain and without relying on a cane to walk. He had no pain in his knees or his feet and knows that Jesus Christ Almighty saved him. PRAISE GOD!!!

Maybe five minutes later, I called my dad to see how his doctor appointment went regarding his foot. He said, "Mary, I walked in there with Pete and told the doctor that he believed God had healed him but that Pete needed confirmation. The doctor said, 'Well, let's see.' The doctor took two X-rays and found no broken bones. Pete said, 'Take another one.' So, the doctor agreed, and still no broken bones, no muscle damage, no torn cartilage, nothing. And again, Pete asked for another X-ray, but again, nothing could be found."

You see, dad was supposed to have surgery before coming to Alaska and was taking the chance by coming to Alaska that the bone would heal incorrectly and would have to be rebroken.

Pete and his wife even called me to try and talk my parents out of coming so that dad would have the surgery. I am so glad my parents followed their faith and came, in spite of what the doctors were saying. Praise God, Pete now knows the power of prayer, too.

Three to four minutes later, my brother Rich called, "Hey, Mary, I want to apologize to you and Vince but mostly to your church. You see, I judged them and your pastor before I knew anything about it. Frankly, I thought the church was weird and I am so sorry. It's different than I have ever experienced, I have never been to a church before where I felt welcomed the first time I walked in. Mary, I am so sorry if I made you or Vince feel uncomfortable or anything."

I told him that our church is not a bunch of judgmental hypocrites, and that that they were used to being labeled as weird, but that I understood what he was talking about. I explained that "weird thing" was the Holy Spirit and that what we grew up in was "religion."

He said, "Mary I don't know that I am as saved as you." I said, "Brother, you simply turned your eyes off of God, but He never turned his eyes off of you. And if you allow the Holy Spirit to move in your life, He would love to share the "weird" with you."

We hung up the phone talking about the Holy Spirit and how His promise never fails.

Jerrod

I first attended services at Ministry of the Living Stones in 2014 and started attending regularly when I moved on to the peninsula at the end of 2018. I met Vickie at one of the first services I went to, and she made an immediate, unforgettable impression. When I first heard her speak from the pulpit, I was taken for a loop. I had never heard anything like it before. She came across raw and genuine, and she spoke with a fire that I had never experienced anywhere else.

Over the years, Vickie has taught me many things about the Word of God and what it means to be a true Christian. My walk as a Christian has benefited tremendously from her constant encouragement, correction, and guidance. Vickie's unyielding dedication to the Lord and His Body, through loss and hardship, has taught me the meaning of endurance and perseverance. Her ability to forgive, pray, and love anyone who comes through the doors, including those who hurt her, has taught me how to be a true servant of God.

The greatest lesson she has taught me came from her never, not once, taking credit for what she has accomplished. She has always given the glory to God. She and the ministry have taught me about what it means to have a true relationship with God and His Son, Jesus Christ. They have seen me through my highs and lows, have forgiven me when I've stumbled, and have never given up on me. I truly owe Vickie and the Body of Christ at the Ministry of the Living Stones my life because without them I would not be saved. I wouldn't be born again, Spirit-filled, and pursuing a victorious, redeemed life in Christ Jesus, my Master, my King, and my Brother.

In the years I have attended MLS, I have witnessed many miracles, signs, and wonders. I have seen bodies healed of injuries and infirmities. I have seen hearts, minds, and lives, that were broken and lost, mended and changed forever. People giving their hearts to Christ is one of the most incredible and beautiful things I have ever witnessed. I still cry with joy every time I see the humility of the penitent and the hope renewed of the forgiven. God has performed miracles in my life as well.

My grandma was diagnosed with bladder and lung cancer in late 2022. After a large cancerous mass was removed from her bladder, further testing showed that the cancers had infected lymph nodes and spread over most of her body. Her oncologist told us that her cancer would not be curable and the best we could hope for was to "manage" it with treatment. Several months into treatment the doctor's prediction had proven itself to be true. The cancer had stopped growing but it was not going away.

At this same time the Ministry of the Living Stones was going through a Holy Spirit-led revival. We were gathering together every night for hours to pray, praise, and worship the Lord God. The anointed Word, confessions, and repentance flowed from the hearts of the members of the Body of Christ.

During the 62 days of this revival, the Holy Spirit led me to pray for my grandma. I anointed her with oil and by the power of the Holy Spirit, the laying on of hands, and our faith, she was healed. Two weeks later her scans showed that the cancer in her lymph nodes and bladder were completely gone and that the spot in her lung had shrunk and become benign.

The doctors were dumbfounded. All the glory was God's.

This is just one of many of the incredible, mountain-moving miracles that being a part of this Body has exposed me to, and I am forever grateful to the Lord God, his servant Vickie, and the Ministry of the Living Stones for it. It is because of them my life has been undeniably and irrevocably transformed for the good.

Amanda

I've known Vickie my whole life. In 35 years, I have seen people set free from demonic oppression, people healed from all sorts of maladies, and hearts changed to follow after God through the power of the Holy Spirit.

She's who I go to when I need Godly advice. Vickie is always pointing us to God and to Jesus Christ; encouraging everyone to search out the things we are told, to build our own relationship with Jesus Christ, and not depend on others to tell you what you should be doing for God. There have been several women in the church who doctors told they could not get pregnant that now after prayer have children.

A changed heart and transformed life is the greatest miracle to see.

Holly

My mom had fallen and broken her pelvis. We had been taking care of her for six weeks. We took her to the doctor for a checkup. The doctor sent us over to the emergency room. The emergency room doctor told us her sodium levels were low, but they could fix her. They admitted her to the hospital and moved her into a room. My sister told Mom goodbye; she would see her tomorrow. I stayed for a couple more hours. Mom fell asleep and seemed to be resting well. I told her I was going home to get some rest.

As I was driving home the hospital called and asked if she had a DNR (Do Not Resuscitate) order, because she was unresponsive.

I picked my husband up from home and we went back to the hospital. I knew the minute I walked into the room that my Mom was gone. My sisters were there with their pastors. I was praying over my mom when Vickie walked into the room and told the people if they didn't have the faith of the four (Matthew, Mark, Luke and John), to leave the room.

Everyone but my husband, my father-in-law, and myself left the room.

Vickie prayed over Mom to wake up in the name of Jesus. My Mom woke up. She said God sent her back; her job wasn't done yet.

Two weeks later, I kissed Mom's forehead and told her I would see her in heaven. She opened her eyes, smiled really big, and went to be with Jesus.

Aaliyah

I met Vickie when I was seven years old, during the time when I was going back and forth between my mom and dad. My dad, who I didn't really know at the time, and my stepmother, Amanda, brought me to church. I heard my grandma on my birth mother's side talk about God before, as well as my birth mom, but we never went to church., So it was a whole new experience for me. I wasn't sure what to think of it at first, being as young as I was.

When I saw Vickie for the first time, I was amazed because she was happy, bold, and knew who she was, especially in Jesus Christ. Over the years, she has taught me so many things, from verbal to physical. Which is an amazing thing, because these days a lot of people are all talk and no action.

I've seen her pray over people and talk with them and I've seen their lives completely change, mine included. She always challenges the way I think, which I'm glad for because it always has me looking into things like I never have before.

The miracles I've seen her do through the Holy Spirit and Jesus Christ in her are also miraculous. Like my Aunt Sierra, for example. The doctors told her for years she couldn't have children, and Vickie had prayed for her and told her she was going to have a child. Then, low and behold, the doctors were proved wrong, and she had a child.

Vickie has shown me that no matter what people or what things throw at you, as long as you trust in Jesus, your best friend and brother who will never leave nor forsake you, everything will work out. You just have to trust Him with your whole heart and be devoted.

Vickie always speaks about how, "being all in and being bold as a lion" is important because that's what Christians need to aim for, to have "that Holy Spirit backbone," which for a while I didn't get, because a lot of people who claim to be Christians are not that way but should be.

As Vickie says, "Bold is gold in the Kingdom of God," which is one of my favorite sayings because it is always a good reminder to take a stand in Jesus Christ, no matter what.

There was a while where I worked for her business, a BBQ food truck. She would come around to visit a lot, and during the first few years of that volunteering I was oppressed for a lot of reasons, thinking I was never good enough. How could I possibly measure up to all these people that do all these amazing miracles and such? Every time she would come around to visit, at the truck, I would learn something that I still carry with me today. Like, for example, she taught me that Christians make mistakes all the time, herself included, and that I just had to repent and move on and not carry it around like baggage.

Over the next couple of years, the more and more I came out of that feeling of oppression. From the time I have spent with Vickie over the years, she's helped me in so many ways to become the young woman of God that I am today, So I'm forever thankful for the God-given compassion and love that she has shown me.

Ralph

I came to this church a complete mess. I was wishy-washy, heady and high-minded, thinking I knew a lot. I was very selfish, always thought about me and how I could get ahead without working hard. My mouth got me into a lot of trouble, I spoke without thinking about others. My flesh ruled me.

This church has shown me to rely on Jesus Christ only. He hears my prayers, and He answers them. It is about the Body of Jesus Christ coming together in the unity of faith and working for a common goal. For all of us to survive, we have to work together.

This church has shown me to look out for others, because Jesus is looking out for me.

Thank you for the opportunity to be part of this Body!

Jennifer

I grew up a pastor's kid, following rules and fitting the part. My parents believed in the power of the Holy Spirit, despite attending an Episcopalian church that frowned upon it. They searched until they attended a conference on fivefold ministry, where as a family, we all met Vickie.

Several years after my sister was sent to live with Vickie and David (her husband), I came to see the place and meet the people of MLS (Ministry of the Living Stones), who changed her. I now know that it was the Holy Spirit that healed her and was drawing me.

During the week of my visit, I saw real love in action. Preachers spending time with the congregation was unheard of to me. The MLS family played softball, went to movies, went out to lunch, rotated shifts at a garage sale for the missions, and in the evenings would gather around and share stories of God's goodness.

That Sunday, I declared to Vickie that MLS would now be my church. I asked the Body to consider me one of their own, and to pray for me while I completed (a voluntary) one year mission commitment to Russia.

One of the first miracles that I experienced was a phone call in the middle of the night. Ignorantly, I had put myself in danger, staying in an unknown place, away from the group. I answered the ringing to Vickie's voice telling me that I was not safe and to leave immediately. Later, I discovered the house was trafficking girls to Morocco.

I returned to Alaska in 1994 where I met my future husband on a softball field. Brian and I were married in 1995. It was a time and season when the people in Body of Christ were inseparable. We had fun! Many of the women began homeschooling and teaching each other's children, so I helped.

The men built a school building where we poured good character into the young lives of kindergarteners through the 12th grade. We prayed, we laughed, we planted seeds. Vickie taught the Word of God, encouraging the insecure; she intuitively knew when there was trouble brewing and a teen needed an "outside the box" answer.

We all maintained the buildings. We painted, raked, and removed snow. I knew that I had a real job...but I don't even remember it taking much of my time. I was always with the Body of Christ!

In the year 2000, my 4-month-old son died of SIDS. I could have been one of the many people that succumbed to their devastation. But the mercy and grace of God met me. Vickie and the body of Christ stepped in to strengthen and speak truth even when we didn't understand the "whys?"

Later that year, Vickie started another mission in Brazil, and I wanted to help her start a school there. We offered English not only to children, but to the men who needed to advance within their companies to support their families. God used that gift to bring people into a church and into his Kingdom.

Vickie has counselled numerous couples in their marriages. She helped to save mine with some simple advice, "You can't control how he will react." Ultimately, I wanted God to save my marriage, but I had wanted my husband to feel my pain as some kind of penalty. Had I gone with my fleshy "wants," we would not be married today. Only God can change a heart.

I have witnessed God's healing power through Vickie. Many have come to church with canes, crutches, braces, and left walking on their own. My dad was in a car accident, unresponsive, before the Jaws of Life removed the door to rescue him, Vickie prayed, and he came alive. My sister was deaf, and in an instant could hear the praise and worship, healed by the anointed of God, Vickie. My knee was hyperextended when I slipped on the ice. I heard the pop and could not put any weight on my leg. I went to church that night during a season of 62 days straight revival prayer. I hobbled to the front to pray.

"Do you believe that the same power that raised Jesus from the dead can heal you?" "Yes" I replied. So, Vickie asked me to walk up the five steps toward the cross. I did. Then, I walked down the same five steps and continued walking in God's healing.

God planted me at Ministries of the Living Stones where I could grow and learn His ways.

Dominique

I am beyond blessed to have been a part of Ministry of the Living Stones my entire life. I was born and raised in this church, and because of this, have known Verissa Walber (Vickie) just as long. The impact Vickie has had on my life is immense. I would need more than one letter to tell all the things. Here are only a few things that I have been able to learn, witness, and be a part of: I was exposed to the presence, anointing, and power of God that rests in this church since I was young. I have both seen and personally experienced healings and miracles, most of them through Vickie's hands by the power of God. I was a child with constant infirmities, from broken bones to autoimmune diseases, and God has healed me of them all!

The first one I remember: I was about 7 years old and came to church in a full cast on my leg. Vickie walked up to me during praise and worship, knelt, grabbed my leg, and began to pray. I physically felt my bones realign and was able to walk without the cast or crutches. Praise Jesus!

Another time, I was 17 years old in Israel, Vickie baptized me in the Jordan river. She also prayed for complete healing for my body. I didn't know until months later when I went in for my already scheduled surgery, that the hip labrum tear I had for five years was completely healed, and my blood work for the all of the autoimmune diseases came back completely negative. I have never had an issue since!

I've received healing in so many other ways! One being spiritual deliverance! During the end of a service, whole praise and worship was continuing, I was receiving prayer and went into full possession. I remember it all so clearly. Vickie had just left the church. It was at the end of the service and there were a few others remaining for praise and worship. So many people were laying hands on me, praying for me, pouring oil on my head, putting a Bible on my hands, all while this demon was tossing me around like a rag doll. I was in pain, I had zero control of my body, and I was scared. I prayed to God to either get this thing out of me or take me home.

As soon as I prayed, I saw Vickie's face above me. She laid hands on me, commanding the demon to leave, and it did immediately. She loved me enough to drive back to the church. She understands and walks in the authority that God gives her, and because of that God-given authority, deliverance and healing take place. I am free by the power of God, and Vickie was the yielded vessel God used to free me.

I've traveled to several nations with Vickie and have seen her do all these things and more with so many others. She trusts the Holy Spirit and believes every Word He speaks. She walks a life of victory and power because that's the life Jesus Christ has given to her. She takes no credit for herself, knowing that all credit and glory belong to God the Father. Everyone around her hears of Jesus, and she teaches all the congregation to walk with His Holy Spirit!

Marsha

In order to describe the effect Vickie has had on my soul through the Trinity, a little personal history needs to be known.

I was baptized as a baby in water in a Catholic church and raised Catholic by my parents. They insisted I attend a Catholic grade school, Catholic high school, and Catholic college. They were taught Catholic was the true religion and lived by that. It was the only way they knew growing up also. Little did they know, these placements did very little to tame me. I was required to attend weekly masses while I lived at home. As time went on, I felt in my entire being and soul, there must be more to heaven than showing up weekly for mass and going to confession for sins that every human will have.

I never read the Bible because I thought I knew what I needed to know about God from the readings at Catholic masses. The divine role of the Holy Spirit or baptism in the Holy Spirit was unknown to me. I was taught as long as I was baptized as a baby and had the sacraments and obeyed the commandments as best I could, I would go to heaven. I also assumed unless a person chose to be evil, and confess sins, they would also go to heaven, and depending on those sins, a person may have to wait to see God.

Through the years I just had it in me to try to help people, be nonjudgmental, compassionate, and generous. I felt sorry for those who didn't have a lot of those feelings. I thought through my actions towards others that I was doing my part to help teach others the way to live to have an afterlife in heaven. I didn't feel the need to really vocalize the existence of God and Jesus because I didn't relish being "told" what others' opinions were for me to live by.

I came to realize through meeting Luanne, the author of this book, and then through Luanne, meeting Vickie, that the Holy Spirit is a very special part of God and Jesus and this should be vocalized! Before meeting both of these phenomenal women and servants of Jesus, I encountered a miracle when I was in my 30s. I was very sick for years with chronic fatigue syndrome. No medication would help. I continued my life and prayed often it would leave me. I was a big partier most of my life, starting at the age of 16...something had a hold of me, but I realize I was also very protected from heaven!

One late afternoon after work, I entered one of my favorite restaurant/bars to meet friends, and I felt this lifting from my feet all the way up over my head, and I was no longer sick. I started crying and thanking God with joy, telling everyone I knew what had happened. I didn't think miracles could happen like that, and I was set on a new path!

I met Luanne, the author of this book, through my business, and she guided me on my new path. Then, Luanne introduced me to Vickie, and I now see the Holy Spirit and God and Jesus in the most glorious light!

Vickie has an undeniable halo around her that demands precious attention. She directs you to the Trinity without being overbearing – just with immense love! You can feel it ooze from her on how much richness can be received from the Trinity if we just trust and have faith.

Through Jesus by the power of the Holy Spirit, my mom and I both were healed with Vickie's prayers. I have since been baptized in the Holy Spirit, I read the Bible and other books of divine inspiration and have become part of a fivefold ministry to continue to help others to find Jesus. The only way to get to heaven is through Him!

Vickie is truly a handmaiden of the Lord! I know I have found sisterhood in Vickie and Luanne and strive to make heaven proud of me. I love them both and know I was put in their path for my continued journey!

Anonymous

I met Vickie in 1992 in Oklahoma. She was with a group of Alaskan men and women preaching there. That's where I formed a relationship with her and the group. Vickie brought me back to Jesus Christ. I was living a rotten life, and she showed me what it was to be a real Christian. So, I eventually moved to Alaska, and I knew this was the place I needed to be.

Through all the years, my walk with Jesus Christ was growing and getting revelations through Vickie. I always thought of myself as a loser, no ambition, low self-esteem, but Vickie saw right through me and saw something in me. She never gave up on me. Every time I was going through a rough patch in life, Vickie was right there beside me.

In early 2000, me and my wife lost a three-month-old baby. Vickie helped us through it. Whenever I wanted to give up on everything, Vickie was encouraging to get going. She would not let me stop.

Since I have been in Alaska I have seen tons of miracles. Deaf people hear, marriages are restored, people coming into church with crutches and leaving them behind.

Vickie restored my marriage. I was on the edge of divorce, but she prayed and counseled us and to this day my wife and I are still taking a walk with each other.

I know that Vickie is a woman of God by her actions. She is showing us what it takes to follow Jesus Christ in all the ups and downs in life.

Paige

I never truly understood the true love that God freely gives, because growing up I always thought I had to do something to earn any type of love, until I started going to MLS six years ago. Being raised by a single mother, she let me know that my father abandoned me before I was even born. When I reconnected with him over the phone and e-mail, he made it abundantly clear that he never wanted to meet me let alone get to know me.

Growing up, my relationship with church, let alone God, was very superficial. We would go to church with my grandparents from time to time, but all I ever heard was that Jesus died for our sins and that we were never to disobey God by committing a sin. I remember feeling like, "How can I ever be good enough to impress God?"

As I got older, we stopped going to church altogether. It wasn't until I graduated from high school and was living with my boyfriend and his mother that I started to want to seek a relationship with God. At that time, I told her that I didn't believe in God, that I had tried to when I was younger, but it wasn't something I was interested in. She gave me a Bible and told me as long as I was staying with her, I would have to attend church.

I would go out on Saturday night and drink with my boyfriend and his friends until the crack of dawn and she would still make sure to wake me up so that we could attend church. It was a little church that we attended at the Nikiski Senior Center. We would break down verses and I started to want to read and understand the Bible.

Shortly after that, my boyfriend and I broke up. I moved back to Soldotna, but that experience had lit a fire within me to search out God's Word. I thought that if I threw myself in another church, I would continue to grow my relationship with God. Unfortunately, what I didn't know is that not all churches are the same.

I went to a big church in town and found myself lost again. I was surrounded by hundreds of people but felt so alone. I only attended a handful of services before beginning to feel like I would never fully understand the Bible because it was too late and stopped going altogether.

I didn't understand praying at that time, but I always hoped that I would find someone to go to church with and maybe they could help me understand God's Word.

When I met my now husband, he and his friend had told me about a church that they had been going to their whole lives. I thought it was a church that I had attended when I was a child. Oh, how wrong I was. It was nothing I had ever been to.

The moment I walked into the building there was a different type of energy, and although I didn't truly know anyone in there, I felt welcomed. I remember this loud, tall woman speaking and thinking oh she must be the pastor's wife at the church, there were many. That was so different. I was used to one person running the whole show and definitely had never seen a woman preach.

The first day I was there she was upset and speaking to the church very sternly, but I could tell that through her anger it was coming from a place of love. She didn't want anyone to stray from their salvation.

It was as if that fire that was stirring up within me had been doused with kerosene, I wanted more. My husband, who was just a friend at the time, asked me after if I would want to return. I think he thought I would be scared away by the service, but he didn't know... this was the first time I had felt so welcomed.

Paul

I was born in the church and from what I remember I truly met Vickie when I was four or five years old, she has taught me a lot in the past 27 years of attending MLS. I remember her teaching us that we need to search out a matter and not take what she said at face value. To this day, we still get told to get in our Bibles and find out for ourselves the truth about who we are in Jesus Christ. The biggest part about that is believing in what we were reading. I also learned that it's not only believing, but also walking out the Word of God.

I learned being a Christian is not an act but a way of life I learned from Vickie that none of us are special and hearing her testimony on how she met Jesus Christ was amazing to me. Since hearing her testimony, I believe God will take what the world calls "not qualified" or "not smart enough" and use them to serve in His Kingdom.

The biggest thing I learned though was that we can do nothing without God but in Him we can do anything.

The first miracle I got to witness was a family that had infertility issues. They were told they would not be able to have any babies. That Sunday, Vickie had prayed over her and told her she would be pregnant. Before you know it, the woman that was told she could not have babies had three babies. I believe I was 10 years old at this time. I was hooked, and there was and still is nothing that could tell me God wasn't real.

I, myself, had bad growing pains when I was growing up. It got to the point I had to use crutches. I remember getting a call from Vickie and she was talking to my mom, and she handed the phone to me. Vickie asked me, "Do you believe God can heal your growing pains?" I said "Yes." She then said without hesitation, "Drop the crutches and walk by faith."

So, I did, and as I did, the pain instantly went away. I remember understanding that faith was just doing and believing, which is what I did by dropping those crutches and grabbing on to faith.

A lot has changed for me since then. My parents, who had been together for a long time, had gotten a divorce. If I had chosen to stay with my mom, I would not be here anymore in MLS.

Now, growing up, it was always my dad and I reading the Bible every day for at least an hour or so. My Mom never really took part in that because it made her feel convicted. From what I learned from my dad is, "Without conviction there would be no change."

God is never-changing but we should be in Him. In that, I felt that my dad and I had always a close bond with one another, and we agreed on the Word of God.

Fast forwarding to the divorce, he said he will never lie to me, and I would not to him.

When I was talking with my mom, I asked why she wanted to divorce my dad. She replied and said, "I do not love your dad," and stayed with him because he made her feel safe.

At that moment, I realized that was not my mom, at least that's what I felt like. I felt lied to by her because she promised me things would work out. I chose my dad to have full custody over me when I was 16 years old. The reason why I decided that was because one of two things, he would not lie to me, and I knew if I stayed with him, I would be fed the Word of God and be told the truth about who I am in Jesus Christ.

Stephen

I met Vickie Walber in January of 1994. I had just moved back to the Kenai peninsula a few weeks prior in December with my wife and two young boys. My mom, sister and brother-in-law invited me to come to church at the Ministries of the Living Stones.

The moment I walked through the door I felt the presence of God so powerfully. I grew up in churches my whole life without feeling the presence of God, so this was totally new to me.

I've been working with Vickie hand in hand for the last 30 years. I have been her praise and worship leader for 28 years. I've visited 4 foreign countries with her: Costa Rica, Nicaragua, Israel, and Africa.

Personally, Vickie has been such a blessing to me and my family. She has given me 30 years of Biblical counsel. I was having problems in my marriage and her counsel was what we needed to work things out. Happy to say I've been married for 35 years.

I've never met anyone who is in tune with the Holy Spirit more than Vickie. I call her Vickie, Mom, Teacher, and Friend. I love her dearly, and I'm so thankful to God for putting us together for ministry.

Michael

My name is Michael, and I am striving to become a new man, changing every day. Two years ago, I met Vickie Walber, a woman who has shown me what it means to be a man of God. She explains spiritual truths in a way that resonate deeply with me, making them applicable to my daily walk.

I lived in Arizona, where I had the pleasure of meeting my beautiful wife, Briana. She grew up in the church, and after a few years in Arizona, one recurring theme was evident: She needed the church. No other church could compare; we tried, but to no avail. There was a definite void that needed to be filled and a drawing to the only One who could provide the answer. Little did I know that it was all part of His plan. God's hand was guiding me, even when I was unaware. I came because it was His will. Left to my own devices, I was lost, but He was always leading me.

Vickie's voice carries further than most, filled with the Holy Spirit and speaking with such power. Her belief is so strong, and her testimony is so moving, that I saw many parallels to my own life. I had to see it for myself. Despite everything she's been through, if she hadn't shared her story, I would never have guessed she had walked that path. Vickie speaks life. She's honest. Always searching for a way to better your life. She's a woman of God—a woman I pray and see my wife becoming beside me, changed in all of His glory.

The first time I went to MLS it scared me—well, not literally, but my soul rebelled. It fought harder than ever before because it knew it was threatened. I realized then that I had been chosen. I had been fighting and questioning, lukewarm at best, never fully giving my all. My knee would not bend; I was still serving myself. But slowly, I began to yield, letting go of one fleshly desire at a time as He removed them.

One miracle I've witnessed firsthand in the church was God removing barriers in my life. We prayed for favor to get my license back to relieve stress on transportation. Everyone said He could do it, and I watched in amazement as I refreshed the State's website, seeing stipulations disappear as if they had been met. I couldn't believe it—I didn't believe it.

I called 3 or 4 different divisions, and they all confirmed that I was in compliance (with all laws and regulations). I hadn't done anything; God did it in a millisecond. You better believe I was rattled. How could this be? Why am I changing? Does God really have a plan for me?

If that wasn't enough, six months later, we were blessed with our fourth child, Ezra. He was born deaf and had many other ailments. We prayed—I prayed and prayed. The church prayed. Vickie laid hands on him, we anointed him with oil, and we prayed with such fervency. He was healed. Truly amazing. I was healed as well—of perversion, hate, lust, and envy. I was given eyes of compassion and a mind to match.

I could name countless other miracles and blessings that have happened within the church for my brothers and sisters in Jesus Christ. MLS will either have you running for the hills, forever haunted by the void it leaves, or it will have you daily examining your life choices, bettering yourself, and breaking generational curses to give your children a head start.

I can say that I have noticed a difference—not just in the things God has removed from my life, but in the way I think, the way I see others, and the way I see myself. I have grown into the person I needed as a child. I've become my own hero through God.

MLS, Vickie, and all its working parts are just what you see…I would encourage you to come to MLS to witness the unseen, to be amazed and rewarded with an everlasting life with Jesus Christ, our Lord and Savior.

Thank you.

Briana

I met Vickie when I was 9 turning 10 years old. I come from a past of extreme mental, physical/sexual abuse. At that time, I was passed from a few families and was coming into a new household. They had my biological brother and so it was a chance I had at a new life.

Even from a young age, I knew something was different about Ministries of the Living Stones. The Holy Spirit is very much alive there and the community and the church body is what you would expect as is commanded in the Bible. I witnessed many deliverances and miracles as a child with Ministries of the Living Stones. Before I left, we made a film called *48 Below*, and it won the Spirit Award in Hollywood by the power of God.

When I was 14, my biological mother called and made many promises, so I moved to Arizona to live with her in 2011. My biological brother soon followed, but he lost his life in 2020 due to a long battle of drugs and complications.

At that point, I was headstrong to try and get home, but I had many obstacles in my way. Out of the blue, God made a way where there seemed to be no way and I had finally a way to get home; He removed the obstacle.

In March of 2022, I got to come home to MLS. I had been wanting to be home for so long. I was depressed and anxious and I had severe PTSD. I was on meds for it, and in therapy for it, but nothing was helping me. I was in a horrible place in my marriage, and I was ready to end my life. I just knew that if I got home, I could be saved. I had that in my heart for years.

Like the woman with the flow of blood in the Bible who just knew if she touched Jesus' garment she would be healed, that was all I wanted for so many years. So, two months after being home, a service was held and there was a deliverance happening. I knew that was my chance, and I ran to the front. I threw my arms in the air and cried out with my Spirit, I just wanted to feel alive again and like everything would be okay.

Vickie came to me to pray for me. She commanded it to leave, and I literally felt from the top of my head something go down my whole body and out of my feet, it hit the floor, and I felt this weight just gone and away from me like I could breathe again and she said that I would feel joy finally for literally the first time in my life, and she was right! I was laughing, I was crying, and I just couldn't understand, this foreign feeling was so freeing. I looked outside at the wind in the trees, and I felt I could see beauty for the first time. I felt secure and on fire for God.

Since then, I have seen and witnessed many miracles in the church. Women who couldn't have babies have had babies. Lives totally transformed, and demons delivered from them. There are too many things to count, too many miracles.

Personally, my marriage has been restored, my financial situation finally stable where I never thought it would be. I was hemorrhaging in the hospital and having complications giving birth, but Vickie came and prayed, and God came, healing me.

My son was born deaf, and he was healed and delivered of that. My son couldn't eat, and he is finally eating. My son couldn't move his body well and he's finally learned to crawl and move.

I've seen bones healed before my eyes, knife accidents that didn't even leave a mark, skin conditions cleared, and elderly disabled folks jump with praise. I finally got to a place in my life where I could find peace and not constantly feel like I'm in fight or flight mode/ survival mode.

Vickie has been a huge role in my spiritual life. She has helped me to understand and overcome with the power of the Holy Spirit. She has helped me to understand where fear, oppression, gluttony, self-hatred, abandonment, rejection issues, and self-doubt come from.

I was able to forgive myself for the things that I have done in my past, and she helped me to understand that I am a new creation, that the old me is dead. She's helped me to be bold in Jesus Christ and to let go of the past. She's helped me realize what is truly important in life and that the rest is all filler and distractions.

She helped me realize that because I am a willing vessel for God, because I believe every Word He says, because I am filling myself with the Word of God and trying my best to do God's will in my life, that makes me qualified for lack of a better word. That makes me enough.

I thought that I couldn't minister or travel for God because I was so damaged, but after understanding that my testimony can help to set free others like me, or from similar situations, that helped set me free further. She helped me understand that we are exactly where we are supposed to be, it's not a race, and not to compare ourselves to others, to trust God to take you and use you as He sees fit, not how we see fit. Vickie taught me how God uses the least likely, and she helped me to be proud to be a remnant!

True surrender is a completely different thing than just giving your heart to God. It's trusting Him with your whole life, regardless of what it looks like, because as I stated before...it's all just filler and distraction. So, losing something, and so forth, may seem unfair or whatever at the time, but you don't know God's plan for your life. So, rejoice in the trials and what you see as losses...count it all as joy and blessings. The JOY of the Lord is my strength (Nehemiah 8:10)...I finally understand that because of Vickie and her leadership.

Vickie is the reason I wanted to come home so badly. She's the reason I fought so hard for it...I realize now that it's God IN HER and the Holy Spirit that drew me to her the whole time. I've grown to love Vickie for who she is. She taught me the power of life and death we have in the tongue through the Holy Spirit and the importance of speaking life.

Vickie is as bold as a lion, she's honest and faithful in all things. No one is perfect but she lives her life as I imagine Jesus did. I will never be the same because of who she is and her testimony, and I will forever be inspired and strive to do the same.

There is power in the name of Jesus and there is no limit on what God can do! All you need is faith the size of a mustard seed—how beautiful!

Dusty

I have known Vickie for 34 years. She has been a great example of how I would like to live my life the whole time. She has shown me what it means to be a steadfast and fervent child of God. I have witnessed many miracles of both physical and spiritual in nature. She has always been a great mentor and teacher of the ways of God and how a person should live their life. She has allowed me to live in her home and taught me ways to help others in their time of need.

There are so many examples of the ways that Vickie has helped me through all the years. I was in a spot when she came and picked me up and rescued me from a family member who was trying to hurt me. I was running through the woods to get away from them, and she sent someone to come get me while they were talking to another person.

There was a time later that I had moved to another city, and she came to visit me almost every week, and helped guide me back from making bad decisions with my life. She would pray with me anytime I needed it and would never push me away.

Vickie has always chosen to help those around her. She helped some of the people I grew up with that had just robbed her. This shows the love she has for them and the ability to forgive them even when their actions were so egregious. She has taken family members of mine when they needed help to get out of jail due to their own mistakes, so they could continue to support their family and try to get help with addictions they had.

Vickie has always been willing to help those around her and love them without conditions. I have seen miracles of people so sick that Vickie has put them in her own bed and after resting in her bed while she stayed in another room they were healed. I have witnessed her praying for others as they were in so much pain they could not walk, and they get up after and can move and exercise without pain.

She has always been willing to pray and help those around her all the time. She will stop everything she is doing when help is needed and go to where the help is needed and do everything that she can to help.

Vickie has taught me to be a better person, child of God, and parent in all the years that I have known her. I have always been able to call her as a mom and have loved her for years. She will always be a family member, and I will never forget all that she has done for everyone around her. The guidance and understanding imparted into my own life has been invaluable even when I was young and did not listen, it was always given.

Vickie has been a pillar in my life, and I will be eternally grateful for everything she has imparted into my life.

Rachel

I met Vickie in 1987 when Marty and I were seeking a new church to attend. A church where the leadership spoke the truth and didn't pander to the flesh of the congregation. Vickie and her sister Celeste would put groceries in our car and Marty decided to see what kind of church they attended and, 37 years later, I am still a part of Ministry of the Living Stones.

When I first started going to MLS, I would only communicate with my husband through sign language or whispers. I would not look at any one in the face, choosing to keep my head down. Even though I still struggle with fear of man, and being a "man" pleaser, I have come a long way. I can have conversations with people without looking at their feet. I have attended college and obtained a degree and managed a convenience store for a number of years.

 Over the 37 years of attending MLS, I have witnessed several people receiving prayer. Women who were unable to have children, through the obedience of Vickie laying hands on them combined with their faith in God, all these women now have children. Another lady, who lost her hearing, can now hear again. Broken hearts, healed. Broken families, reunited. There are so many more miracles.

I learned, no matter what happens in my life, to keep my eyes on Jesus and not the situation. He has always been there, using Vickie when needed, to lead and direct my path.

I am still learning and growing in Jesus Christ.

Philip

My name is Philip and I've known Vickie my whole life, 25 years to be exact. She raised/taught my mom from when she was 14 years old to an adult. To this day, she hasn't stopped.

I have attended MLS as long as I can remember and then some. Since being in the church, I've seen countless things happen. I have seen those with broken limbs be healed. People who were losing their sight, gain it back. The deaf received their hearing.

My mother had always been hard of hearing since she was born and was supposed to be fully deaf by 13 years old but ended up going deaf in her 30s. She was deaf for 8½ months. MLS was having a three-day conference with a guest speaker from Africa. My mom went, reluctantly, and ended up going up and got prayed over. She always describes it as someone slowly turning the music up on the radio.

I, in my own life, have been and still am grateful and blessed to have Vickie in my life. I've always looked to her as a grandmother in my life, as someone who, in the last few years, has really helped me as I have struggled with my faith and walk with God. She has been a huge encouragement for me and even recently has helped me to realize things in my life that I was doing, or didn't realize I was doing that were wrong and has helped me to understand.

Even though I still seem to struggle, I find myself more and more wanting a better relationship with God. It's because of Vickie, the church, and Jesus Christ in them that I am where I am today. Without them I honestly don't know where I'd be. They are...we are family.

I didn't truly realize that until February 22nd, 2022, when my wife and two daughters were in a horrific car accident. My one-year-old (almost 2) was right at the point of impact, and she practically walked away from it. She had a broken arm and bumps and bruises. She's four years old now. She just started preschool and is fiery and sweet.

My wife and youngest baby were flown to Providence hospital in Anchorage where they were put on life support. My youngest was pronounced brain dead on the 24th of February, and donated her organs on the 27th, saving 3 lives. My wife was taken off life support on March 4th and passed away 90 minutes after.

Throughout all of this, I was never alone. The church was pretty much rotating people through and making sure I had everything I needed. My sisters took care of my daughter through all of it. Vickie was out of the State at the time, but she called and left a voicemail. In it she prayed for me and my family, and I just felt peace.

Most of all I know without a shadow of a doubt that God was with me and those that were there strengthened us all throughout that time. I am beyond thankful for all of MLS and I'm proud to call them family.

Louis

God brought Vickie into my life through friends that I was staying with at the time. I didn't want to go at first. I only went because the young woman I was interested in had been encouraging me to go. Little did I know that God was using Amanda to bring me into his Kingdom and meet the woman who would be instrumental in changing the course of my life forever.

Meeting Vickie for the first time, I had never met a woman so bold, so strong in my life. She broke every stereotype about women in church I had learned. I was amazed, and also slightly terrified. Her commanding presence was something I had never experienced before. At the time, I had no idea what it was; that it was the anointing, God's power and authority that was resting on her life.

She asked me if I knew who the Holy Spirit was after church, I had no idea what she was talking about. At the time, I had a vague memory of grandpa mentioning it, but I had no idea that it was He and He was a gift from God, a 2000-year-old promise of a friend that would never leave you or forsake you. A true friend, something that I had lacked my whole life.

I came into the church with a lot of baggage from a religious household and a troubled school life, and an abusive relationship. I didn't know that God could heal a broken heart then free someone from depression or quiet someone's fears, that he cared about the smallest of our needs and wants. That, miracles still happen outside the pages of the Bible.

To be honest, I really didn't know who God was at all, not really. Through the years, I have watched God use Vickie time and time again to defy the reports of doctors. When the doctors told women they could not get pregnant, the women had children. I remember when Phyllis, a member of our church, was diagnosed with cancer. The report from the doctors was not good. She had breast cancer, but that didn't move Vickie off her faith. She prayed for her. A few weeks later, we got the report that she was cancer-free.

A similar thing happened to another member and friend of the church, Kim. I watched her lose all her hair and go through the process of chemo treatments. Vickie encouraged Kim as she went through this terrible ordeal, eventually ending with Kim's healing, not by the hand of the doctors, but through the power of God through Vickie and the church's prayers.

There are many more, but these mentioned here are special to me because I have lost an aunt and my mom's sister to cancer prior to coming to the church. It showed me that miracles and healings are real.

Vickie has taught me how to love. But I would like to discuss the one that is closest to my heart. She taught me that love is kind, it doesn't boast about itself. That love is forgiving people who hurt you even when you don't want to. Even when you are like that, it hurts more than you can bear. She taught me that love that forgives isn't about the person you are forgiving, it's about you letting go of that hurt and giving it to Jesus, that love is loving someone enough to tell them they are going in the wrong direction in life, that God has a better way and a better plan for their life, that love is caring about where someone spends their eternity, that the love of God is merciful, but it is also just.

Love is giving compassion when needed, but also confronting someone's way of thinking, so they may change. The willingness to be hated so that someone may wake up to the truth about what is going on in their life, so they may be free to seek after God to be free from their bondage.   God directs Vickie how to work with every member of the church body and that, to me, is a miracle in itself to know how to approach every member of the body of Jesus Christ here, to hear from God what their spiritual needs are.

God has used Vickie in my life to help with my spiritual needs time and time again. He has used her to deliver me from my spiritual oppression. I was oppressed by demons for many years. I would hear voices other than my soul trying to convince me to harm myself. They would affect the way I would interact with people, distort the way I saw people, but one by one, when the time was right, God would use Vickie to deliver me from my spiritual tormentors.

A tree must be pruned before it is ready for harvest. Pruning doesn't feel good, but the end result is always worth it. God corrects those He loves. That's honestly the biggest thing I am most grateful for is Vickie continues to teach me how to love the way God intended us to. To me, there is no greater lesson.

Francine

I first met Vickie Walber about 10 years ago, when I first began attending Ministry of the Living Stones (MLS). Since first coming to MLS, I have witnessed countless miracles and have seen how God has used Vickie to perform such miracles.

The miracle of my salvation that God used Vickie to perform in my life has been without a doubt the most life changing and saving thing I have witnessed/experienced. God has used Vickie to save those lost in a dying world and brought the word of God to so many looking for answers that only He has.

I was one of those lost in the world, but God had a plan. When I finally moved to Alaska, I was suffering with chronic pain. I had gone through surgery and many medical tests. I had accepted that this was my life. I could not stand or sit for long periods of time. I could not run and was the most comfortable laying down, but even then, I was in a great deal of pain with muscle spasms.

At times, it felt as if my bones were going to rip out of my leg. My sister told me, or rather asked me, "Why don't you ask God to heal you?" It had never occurred to me that God would. I knew that I was a sinner, and I did not think that I was worthy to be healed by God. I began to pray for God to heal me, and at the end of the next service at MLS, God used Vickie to lay hands on me and to heal me. For the first time in two years, I did not have any pain. I have not had any pain since that day that Vickie laid hands on me and prayed for me. I got off of the floor pain free and healed.

God healed me that day through the hands of Vickie Walber.

Dakota

I first met Vickie three years ago when I started attending MLS. Before my first service, my friend Audrey told me it wasn't like other churches, and I just went along with what she said until I actually experienced it.

Through Vickie's teachings, I've learned what the Holy Spirit really is, as well as speaking in tongues is a gift everyone can receive. I knew about it, but never knew that we can receive it. I heard about speaking in tongues and had seen one person who could "speak" them, but no one had ever told me I could or how I would be able to.

Vickie's bold and enthusiastic teachings are not cookie-cutter sermons, they are "tell you how it really is" types that get you thinking and wanting to read the Bible to see for yourself what it says. It is clear she cares about everyone's souls and salvation.

In my time at MLS, I've heard many testimonies of people being healed. I've seen people go up and ask for prayer, but two that stick out to me are a personal experience, and one I got to witness firsthand.

The first one, Mary's parents came to a service one Sunday and after the service was finished everyone who wanted prayer had come to receive it. Mary's dad walked up with crutches and a boot on his foot, received a healing, and then walked without the boot or the crutches.

My personal miracle happened when I had hurt my wrist while I was working. I could hardly move it, let alone lift anything without it hurting. I had prayed for it, but it persisted to hurt. After one Wednesday service, while at Cooks, Louis prayed over it, and the next day I had no pain.

A personal testimony I have is how I came about meeting Audrey, and in turn coming to MLS. I was jobless at the time and in real need of something I could pay the bills with. A friend of mine had sent me a job opening for a new posting at the hospital for a Safe Companion. I wasn't going to apply due to not having my BLS certification, but my friend assured me that the hospital would help me get any license or certifications I needed. So, I applied and got an interview.

The interview wasn't like any typical interview. They hardly talked about the job and only asked me questions about myself. There weren't any questions like why I want to work at the hospital or what my strength and weaknesses are. I was a little surprised that I did get the job and I worked in that position for a year, living paycheck to paycheck, when my friend who was hired after me said he was going to do the CNA course at the college.

I decided I was going to do it with him partly due to me needing money, as well as wanting to help the patients more than what I could do as a safe companion. To be accepted into the course, you had to take a reading and writing test. I didn't have to take them due to my college classes.

After I turned in the paperwork needed, the counselor told me I still had to talk with the instructor, so I asked where the room was, so I knew where to go once I got the call to set it up. The meeting and the instructor were there, so I was able to talk to them right then and there. Afterwards, they told me I was accepted into the class. Once I had my license, I applied for a CNA position and was given it without an interview.

I then soon met Audrey, and we hit it off immediately. She invited me to a Sunday service and I have been going ever since. At the time I didn't think much of it, I was just focused on living, but after meeting Audrey and attending MLS, I've come to the realization that it was all God's plan and that I'm now where He wanted me to be.

MLS is a living church and all who have been called there have been blessed to receive the teachings of Vickie.

Melissa

My name is Melissa, and I have attended MLS church for at least 12 years. I first met Vickie back in 2011 or 2012. It was amazing walking into a Holy Spirit-filled church for the first time. My body would get random vibrations, that were calming but still made me wonder ... what's going on?

I don't remember what Vickie was speaking on that night. However, I do remember her—her boldness, directness, friendliness, and leaving the service not feeling judged.

All the years I have known Vickie she has imparted a lot to me through her preaching and conversations. She helped me to receive the Holy Spirit, and I just took off speaking in tongues, something I wanted forever, it seemed. But I couldn't wrap my "religious mind" around it. She showed me how to reach deep, when I didn't think I could, going through my divorce. Jesus was all around me, I had to stay focused. Vickie was one of my big advocates in my corner making sure I never lost sight of that.

There are so many things I have learned and am still learning. I would have to say though, one of the big ones is this—serve, pray, and get out of the Lord God's way and what He needs to do. Since being a member of MLS, I have witnessed miracles and experienced my own; being told by doctors that I could not get pregnant after Travis and I decided we wanted a family.

I received prayer from Vicki. I still remember it like it was yesterday. Walking up to her, while she was at the front of the church and telling her that Travis and I were ready to have a baby and can she pray over my womb? As soon as her hand touched my stomach it felt like sparks and jolts inside. I knew instantly the Lord God touched and healed my womb. It was only a few months later we were pregnant with our first child of two children.

Vickie Walber is an amazing woman of God. I am grateful to be planted at my church; grateful for mercies to put me in such an amazing place to grow!

Janine

My name is Janine, I met Vickie Walber in 1994. She came to a church that I was attending in Salem, Oregon, called the Church of the Holy Spirit. She was a guest speaker there. My first impression of her was that she was not like any other person that I had ever met. She moved and spoke with authority and there was something different about her. She was not like any other preachers that had come to speak at the church. Shortly after my encounter with Vickie, I chose to move to Alaska, and there I joined the Ministry of the Living Stones.

I have seen God move mightily through Vickie. I remember one time, when we were at the end of a service, she asked if any one needed prayer and a young woman went up for prayer. She was deaf and she wore hearing aids. Vickie placed her fingers in the woman's ears, and she regained her hearing.

I remember on a trip to Israel in 2017, we were crossing into Jordan, and I had a severe asthma attack due to an allergic response to an essential oil a person was using sitting near me on the bus. I remember getting up and running towards the front of the bus gasping for air, trying to get off the bus to breathe. Vickie stopped me, slapped her hand on my chest, and told me to breathe. There was like a shockwave through my chest. I was able to breathe, it took a little bit, but I was able to take deep breaths without the need of an inhaler, I was able to breathe.

Also, during the trip in 2017, it hadn't rained in Israel for several years. Vickie stated to our guides and to the whole group that it would rain by the time we left Israel. As we boarded the plane and were waiting to depart, it started to rain.

On a personal note, Vickie has spoken into my life in a lot of ways. She has given me words of wisdom from God that has helped my walk and changed my heart. God has used her to answer prayer in a way where she has come and spoken words to me that were answers to prayer; there was no way that she would know because it was a conversation between God and myself, but God used her to bring the answer to me.

She has, through counselling, helped me to let go of hurts and offenses from the past so that I can move forward in my walk with

God. She has, through laying of hands, set me free from insecurities and set me free from fear.

Vickie continually encourages me to let go of worldly hooks that are hindering my walk.

Rusty

I met Vickie through my sister and have been in the church 28 or 29 years. I have seen two people delivered from demons and have seen people come into the church on crutches and go out walking. My wife was healed of herpes before they had any drugs that could help. In fact, for me to have a wife and kids was a miracle, I came to the church thinking it would never happen. I have been on mission trips and have seen a man that couldn't walk, and Vickie prayed for him and then he was running around in Nicaragua.

Vickie prayed for my back, touched it, and I felt something move and the pain went away.

The fact that I am still in the church to this day is due to Vickie, for she is genuine and God has used her in my life to set me free. She is the wisest person in Jesus Christ I have ever known, God only gives the best, and she is the best.

I came into the church an introvert and would leave as soon as church was over, I wouldn't talk to anyone I didn't trust anyone especially women, go figure, God would bring me to this church.

I was raised by my dad since I was seven years old and there was no affection and in the way he talked to me made me feel like I was a burden and that love was something that had to be earned. I felt I was unlovable, it took a long time, but I realized Vickie really loves me without having to earn it, which also made it possible to accept that Jesus loves me and will not leave me nor forsake me, no matter what but he does want and will use me, He is incredibly merciful and loving. Through Vickie is how I came to trust in that.

Tiffany

My name is Tiffany and I've known Vickie my entire life, 33 plus years. I have seen so many miracles in this church I've been raised up in, I can't even count them all.

The school I went to, (AHL) the Academy of Higher Learning, Vickie started so that the kids, me included, would not only get a good, great education but also learn about God and be safe. That was a miracle to me because not many people think about the safety of kids and true knowledge these days—especially for kids that aren't their own.

Growing up, I just knew if I got hurt or broke something I'd never have to worry because God would take care of me. I never went to the doctor or hospital when I broke something or injured myself seriously because as soon as my parents prayed over me, I believed and I was healed, and if I still had hurt or pain left, I'd go to church. God used Vickie to pray for me and since I believed, God healed me completely.

The greatest miracle I've witnessed in my life is my heart constantly changing. I've seen God do miraculous things through Vickie. I've seen her cast out demons, heal the sick—both physically and mentally.

I've seen boldness in Jesus Christ, forgiveness, love, grace. All these things actively working in our lives are miracles. Vicki is always there at the drop of a dime and will be whenever called upon, and every time a miracle happens.

Kimberly

I was sexually abused by my father, my uncle, and a female babysitter as a young child. By 2nd grade I wouldn't even allow myself to have dessert because I didn't feel like I deserved it. I wouldn't allow myself to wear anything new for several months because I wasn't good enough to have something new. By age 12 I was having "spells" where my body would shut down and I would relive the abuse, or it would just shut down and I could see and hear but I couldn't talk or move. I was diagnosed with PTSD, developed an eating disorder, was diagnosed clinically depressed, and was suicidal. I was in and out of therapy and treatment centers for this but was still very affected by my issues. Two weeks after I graduated high school, I pressed charges against my dad. I spent the next three years in court. I had to leave college for a while because he would show up there, plus he was watching me with field glasses and kept detailed notebooks of my activity. I continued to struggle with the same mental health issues. My dad ended up going to jail and later was put on probation for ten years.

I ended up getting married, but I couldn't trust my husband with our little girl. It was still causing all sorts of trouble in our marriage, and I was still dealing with the same issues. In 1999, God brought us to Ministry of the Living Stones, through Tina Wegener. God set me free from depression. After six months in church, I got a call from a cousin. They called to inform me that my dad was dying. They also asked that I not tell anyone that they'd called since that whole side of the family had disowned me for taking my dad to court. I didn't know what to do with the information, so I did nothing. I'd spent years in therapy, but all that did was teach me to embrace the hate for my father. They had me throw darts at his picture, run over a blanket that had belonged to him, etc. Hate was all that I had for him. I did not tell anyone about the call, yet someone bought me a plane ticket and another person mailed me $100. I knew within me that this must be God, so I went. I spent the night before I saw him at my mom's house. That night as I was praying, the bedroom filled with a smoke and the peace of God like I had never felt before. I had total peace and knew God was going with me. My mom said that she couldn't get herself to take me, so my grandparents drove me two and a half hours to the hospital where he was. I went into my dad's room alone.

The last time I'd seen him was the last day of court over five years earlier. I had a total peace walking in the room and felt such pity and compassion as my eyes fell on him for the first time. This was not my normal response! My body used to shut down when I saw him before. We had a little small talk and then I asked if he believed in God. He said no. I have to say, I was surprised by his answer! He said that he'd prayed every day, on his knees, for years for God to bring me back into his life and that God never answered his prayer. Despite being in a hospital, in my excitement, I started yelling, "Dad, do you see me standing before you right now? This is YOUR answered prayer! I never wanted to see you again! I hated you! This is your prayer. God just needed to get me in the right place to answer it!"

My dad started to weep. It was the first time I'd ever seen him cry. He asked me to forgive him. He'd never even admitted to what he'd done before that. I got to pray with my own dad, and he asked Jesus into his heart. He didn't end up dying then. There's a lot more to that wonderful story, but for another time. The point was, in all my years of therapy, in all my trying to get past and get over things, I couldn't do it. In my power, I couldn't forgive. In one moment, God took all that pain and unforgiveness and set me free! I was a different person, but I wasn't completely free. Over the years, in the church serving God, He would set me free from things that still held me. Each time, I was so thankful, but I knew that something was still there. There was still a tightness in my chest, and my big test (although I never told anyone) was to try to say the name of Jesus. For some reason it just felt wrong within me to say that name. I would get a twinge of being uncomfortable. It was always still there. I had now been a Christian, a born-again, spirit-filled, tongue-talking believer for 26 years. I sang on the praise team. I served the Body of Christ. I fasted, I prayed, I read my Bible, but I knew something was still not right. Things started to get worse. It became difficult to read. I just couldn't focus anymore and was so easily distractable. My brain had become so foggy and confused over the last several years that it was hard to hold a thought. My thoughts were going so fast that I couldn't remember anything or focus on anything. I have always been a very outgoing, social person, but it was like I couldn't even communicate with others anymore. It was extremely difficult to hold a conversation. I couldn't even think of common words to make a complete thought. I no longer wanted to be around people because it was just too hard. I had gotten really depressed. It severely affected my marriage. I couldn't talk to my husband and was so exhausted all the time.

For years I had an insatiable thirst. I needed to constantly drink water. I was drinking at least two gallons a day. I was literally killing myself, washing out all vitamins and electrolytes from my body. I couldn't fight off infections and was sick all the time. My body was in horrible pain all the time. I'd gone to so many doctors over the years trying to figure out what was wrong with me, but there never seemed to be a reason for all of my symptoms. They finally gave me a diagnosis of fibromyalgia just because of all of my weird symptoms. I was taking different pain medications and an ADHD medication to try to help my brain and thoughts. Nothing seemed to really work though. I still couldn't communicate, was still addled and all over the place, having no peace. I was so tormented all of the time, always questioning myself and could never make a simple decision. I had trouble falling asleep and staying asleep so I never slept well. If I woke up, so did my brain, and I couldn't go back to sleep. Also, the body pain was so bad that I couldn't lie in bed too long. I would often wake up with bruises, often looking like hand or finger prints, all over my body. Finally, my body just shut down. I could hardly walk without help and was living between my bed and recliner. I couldn't even sit in an upright chair most of the time. It even became too much effort and energy to talk. I couldn't work, and I had to close down the home school that I was running out of my house. It had become so hard to read or pray, but every time the doors were open, I was at church. I could do nothing to fix myself. Doctors and specialists could do nothing to help me. God was my only hope. At church He would anoint me and miraculously strengthen my body to stand and sing, but I would leave the anointing and be back to the same way. I kept crying out to God, getting on my face, and pleading with Him to help me.

I had a trip scheduled to go with Vickie and a number of other people to Italy, Greece, and Turkey to visit the seven Churches of Revelation. I continued to ask God for a miracle, not a healing. I needed a miracle. Three days before we left, Vickie called me up to the front of the church and asked how I was doing. She hadn't even touched me when all of a sudden it was like machine gun waves flowing through me from above, through the top of my body to my toes. I did everything I could to stand but then went back under the power of God flowing through me. Vickie said, "I'm not touching you. I want you to know that it was God who healed you."

And He did!

I knew I was healed! I was still easily fatigued though. I hadn't done anything for months. I continued to thank God for healing me and continued to cry out for my miracle, for Him to strengthen my body so I could do this trip! He still hadn't answered me by the day we were leaving. The minute I got out of the car at the airport to leave, God's supernatural strength touched me, and I knew it. I walked miles and miles every day, even up and down hills and mountains with no issues! My strength had been returned, but I still had no peace or clarity of mind. About a week after returning from our trip, Vickie had been in prayer at home when God showed her that I had a demon wrapped around my brain, going down my throat and into my chest with its tail stuck into my heart. He told her that I'd had it since childhood and that it had come in with intense fear and trauma.

The next day at church He reminded her, and she called me down from singing and prayed for me. This thing fought and screamed and jarred me around for what seemed like forever. It had been there a long time! Afterwords, I was exhausted and felt like I had swallowed buckets of glass, but I WAS FREE!

My entire life has changed. The tightness in my chest was gone. Now the big test...saying the Name of Jesus. Nothing! No twinge! I have not stopped saying that name! My thoughts are clear, and I can communicate, and for the first time ever, I have peace! I fall asleep quickly, sleep all night, and can even sleep in. The body pain is gone. Other people have noticed the huge difference in me, saying that I'm still me but not so addled, and I can communicate clearly. I even lost weight and look much thinner. My husband keeps crying and thanking God for giving him his wife back. My insatiable thirst is gone. I now must remind myself to drink water! I had been given Living Water! My energy is still back and increasing. Another surprising benefit is that I've been regular in my bowels ever since I was delivered. I have dealt with chronic constipation my entire life and had to take prescription medication to help with it. I have since stopped that medication and all other medication. I haven't needed them!

I have been a Christian for 26 years. I love God and try my best to serve Him. I knew I still had a demon wrapped up inside of me which God was removing. I don't know why God waited 26 years to set me free. Maybe He had to get me in the right place. Maybe He knew I couldn't handle it all at once. Maybe He wanted to teach me perseverance and to stand in faith. Maybe it was a test. Was He trying to see if I would keep seeking Him? I don't know right now, and I may never know, but one thing I do know is that I am FREE! Thank You, God!

Amy

My name is Amy, and I am writing to tell you about a wonderful woman that God has blessed and honored me with throughout my life.

I met Verissa Walber (Vickie) when I was three years old in 1989. I am now 38 years old. At that time, my mom was a mom of three kids. She was single and had very little to no help. I remember as a child Vickie coming into my mom's and our lives. She was just as dynamic then as she is now.

Throughout the years my mom was married and separated from my abusive alcoholic father. We often would stay at Vickie's. She gave us help and shelter and became just like a grandmother to me and my brothers. Eventually, we moved to live full time with her for about two years. During that time, she tremendously helped my mother, supporting her, praying with her, encouraging her, and building her up in Jesus Christ and his Word. Vickie was and is the very foundation of my mother's, brothers', and my faith in Christ Jesus.

Throughout the many years knowing and growing with Vickie, I have been honored to witness countless miracles and many acts of love and kindness.

I have traveled around the world with her; in Africa, she saved me from a crazy mob of men trying to kidnap me. She wrapped her arm with a sweater and was ready to fight, but thanks to God and the prayer of a righteous women, they could not and did not move.

In Mexico, we started a church together. We were there visiting, and she heard they were in a drought for five years. Vickie prayed that it would rain, and it rained the day we left! The people danced in the rain and beheld a miracle...

Israel—same thing. No rain. Vickie prayed and God sent the rain!

My daughter experienced leg trauma. The doctors were saying multiple fractures and Vickie came to the hospital, prayed, and my daughter was healed.

Now, these are just some personal miracles that I have witnessed with my own eyes. These are physical ones to me that have been a great testament of Vickie's faith and have grown my faith over the years.

I will tell you the greatest honor has been to live, grow, and love—and have Verissa Walber in my life. You want a fighter, a true go-getter, a bull/lion in your corner. Vickie is the one, she will give it 100%, no slack. Her faith is as sure as the river meets the ocean. Her love for God and His people is incomparable. Vickie is a true leader; one I hope to imitate in my life to others and to my own children.

Mikayla

My parents met Vickie and attended MLS when my mom was just 18 years old. I was born into MLS and have seen so many incredible things it's hard to pick. One of my personal favorites carried on into my life.

When I was about 7 years old there was a woman in our church who couldn't have children. She had seen many doctors on the subject and was heartbroken, as she was newly married and desperately wanted to start a family. I watched her come up for prayer and she looked so broken. I remember how hard she cried. Vickie prayed for her and God moved, I saw the peace wash over her. I'm not exactly sure on time since I was so young, but she did end up having children not long after. Over the next few years, she had two sets of twins and one more child.

As an adult, I was told by multiple doctors that I too would be unable to have children. I was told I could go on medication and after five years we could retest to see if it was possible for me to conceive. At first, I cried, then I thought back on that woman and what God did for her.

That next Sunday I ran up for prayer and in my mind, I begged that God would have mercy on me in the same way. I hadn't told anybody except my husband and parents what the doctor said. Vickie came over to me and prayed for me and then she told me that God was giving me a baby. I was so overwhelmed since I had never told her that's what I was asking for. It's funny because I've seen God tell her about many things through the Spirit but for some reason I was surprised.

I left that service knowing without a doubt I would have a baby. A few weeks later, sure enough, I found out I was pregnant with my sweet baby boy. I'm currently pregnant with a little girl. God is so good, and He moves for his people all the time. We just have to give Him the room to do so.

I don't think I could get all the things I've learned from Vickie written down. After all, 30 years is a long time, and she has a complete wealth of knowledge in Jesus Christ. Some things that have really stuck with me over the years are the small things you can do to make the Holy Spirit your friend, how to make him a part of your everyday life, how to dig deep and battle when it feels like all hell is coming at you.

Vickie has overcome some serious battles through Jesus Christ, and I have always felt honored to not only have someone like that as an example, but to have someone like her fighting for me. She truly loves the people God has placed her over.

One of the hardest moments of my life was when my son had been suffering from seizures at three years old. We had taken him to the doctors who told us at this stage there was nothing they could do. They believed he would grow out of them after turning five.

One night, I was woken up like someone was shaking me. I opened my eyes and saw no one so I went back to sleep. This happened two more times. Finally the third time I realized it was God and quickly looked at the screen showing my boy in his room. I saw this creepy looking old lady leaning over him and whispering in his ear.

Growing up in the church, I've seen many demons chased off, so I immediately started yelling in tongues and telling that thing to leave in Jesus name as I ran down the stairs to my son. As I walked in the room, I saw him seizing. I scooped him up and began binding and casting that thing out. I was so loud, I'm sure I terrified the neighbors as I marched around my whole house declaring the name of Jesus and breaking any agreements made with that adversary.

I've never seen any demon leave from a tiny little "please go away," so I got loud and angry, I spoke life over my son and my household. It was an incredible moment for me in Jesus Christ because I've watched these things my whole life but struggled to walk in them.

Vickie had always pushed us that seeing them isn't enough. She had expressed how she is more than willing to pray for us and fight for us, but we need to stand in that authority God has given us and watch the mountains move.

I'm not naturally a loud person, but in this moment, I felt I was fighting for my son, so I fought as hard as I possibly could. I fought in the way that I've seen done countless times by Vickie and the rest of the leadership in our church.

My son was healed from seizures that day, not even one since. Alaska can be a hard place to live for multiple reasons, but I could never leave because nothing could make up for the loss of MLS and the incredible leadership.

Audrey

I have been a part of MLS my whole life. I have known Vickie since I was born. She and Celeste have been a very big part of my life. They have been like grandparents to me. They have always been there for me and encouraged me. I am very thankful that God put them in my life. Vickie has done so much for me spiritually and I am very thankful.

I have witnessed many miracles in my life and others' lives around me through the years. I have seen people healed of cancer, autoimmune diseases, and women's wombs healed so they could have babies. I have seen people set free from all sorts of spiritual bondage.

One thing that has always stood out to me about Vickie is that she always knows what people need to hear through the Holy Spirit. There have been multiple occasions where she has come to me in different ways...she has come to me with stern words, and other times she has come to me very soft and graceful.

One time that I will never forget though was when I was with my ex. There was one night that I was not doing well at all, I was super depressed and hopeless because of this guy. I had let the adversary use him to steal my joy. I had started to become a shell of myself.

Vickie and Celeste randomly showed up to my mom's house to check on me one day to make sure I was okay. That was one of the most encouraging things ever, it made me realize I wasn't alone, God was always watching and there for me even when I didn't feel or see it. God helped me in one of my lowest times and he used them to encourage me.

There have been a lot of times where I have gotten offended with Vickie and how she did things. I used to think it wasn't fair how other people were treated nicer or "got away" with their sins while I was getting called out.

Now that I have matured more in the Word, I realize that it was because of different calls and different giftings. No two people are the same, so why would the correction given by God be the same? He knows what each of us needs to be pushed forward. Sometimes, we need a stern word and other times we need that grace.

There are still a lot of things that God is helping me work out in my life. People-pleasing is something I struggle with a lot, as well as putting myself and other things before God. There are times I have put Vickie and other people on a pedestal in my life, and God has been showing me through Vickie that I can't do that. Vickie is human just like me. I am just as important. The only difference between us is our commitment and the time we spend with God.

Vickie's long-suffering, steadfastness, and boldness is so inspiring. She has always shown me that serving is the greatest thing we can do in the Kingdom of God.

Through the years, I have let the things of the world and other people harden my heart, and I have not served as I used to. God has been bringing me out of that funk and I have been getting my joy back.

I have lost a lot of people very dear to me in the past few years, and it has been very hard on my heart. God brought me my now husband during this time, and I am so thankful for it. My husband, Dakota, has been very encouraging. He reminds me of Vickie's and others' teachings when I am feeling discouraged or lost.

Vickie has done so much in my life, more than I can even fathom. I am very thankful for her and the gift God has placed in her life. Without Vickie and Celeste, I would not be where I am today.

I thank God every day for Vickie, she has been an amazing example of a true disciple of God.

Anonymous

I came to know Vickie Walber through a lady named Joanie. Joanie worked at the federal building in Anchorage, Alaska. She worked in one area, and I was training at BLM. So, we were coming out of the bathroom together one day in March of 1990. She asked me if I would like to come to church with her on a Friday night, and I said yes. I've been going ever since.

One day in a church service, Vickie stood up and looked at me and said she saw me healed. On one of the Sundays, we went to a service, then after that we went to Sandy's house. We were singing in her living room and Vickie said she saw heaven open up and there were alabaster boxes, and they were opened up and wanted to be gifted to us. I said quietly, "I receive it."

Then, a little bit after, we went down to the river and Vickie baptized those who wanted to do so. I was one of them.

After that, we drove back home to Anchorage. When we got home, I was sitting in Joanie's house and just singing to God and looked down and my foot was straight! God had turned my whole leg straight and my hip, too!

I remember one day when we were in the first service in the new church in Sterling, Alaska. Vickie said she saw me praising God and that I was standing before God's throne.

Vickie encouraged me to go to be a nurse. She never gave up on me. I ended taking a CNA course. I found a job and have been working ever since 2010 on November the 11th.

There was someone in the church that had become deaf. Vickie prayed for them, and God came down and touched their ears to where they could hear again.

Vickie helped me put my fire out of my house when it caught fire, along with a couple of other people. We did not even have to call the fire department.

I have seen Vickie pray for people to get set free of themselves and they were delivered, set free more than they have ever been. I have seen someone come in on crutches, and Vickie prayed for them, and they walked out of the church without having the crutches.

Michelle

I moved to Alaska in December of 1994. Little did I know but Vickie and the church had been praying that God would bring me and my family to Alaska. I wasn't raised in church, nor did I attend church. I was raised to not allow people to see your weaknesses. I was so hard-hearted. The first time I attended a church service, it brought me to my knees.

The Spirit of God was so strong on Vickie and all the people in that building, I couldn't contain myself. I cried harder than I ever had in my life. Vickie gave me the words of knowledge that only God knew about and me. I gave my heart to the Lord God that night and never looked back. God pulled my walls down through the teachings of Vickie and Celeste, and reading and praying and fasting.

A few years after we started at the church, my husband committed adultery. Vicki and Celeste came alongside of my husband and me. Through much prayer and counseling we were able to rebuild our marriage and have had a firm foundation in Jesus Christ since then. God healed both of us. We just celebrated 35 years of marriage.

Vickie has worked hard for many of us to go on mission trips. I have gone on a couple of them. This has been such a humbling experience and helped me grow in so many ways.

We have seen so much deliverance and healings over the years. I was in a car accident in my early 20s and injured my back. I then broke my back 20 years later. Vickie prayed for me and God healed me. Her faith has always been so prevalent in my life and the life of so many others.

My husband and I have worked with Vickie on the praise and worship team for many years.

I am so thankful to be a part of MLS.

John and Nicole

God led my wife and me to a little church in Anchorage, Alaska, on 69th St.

We walked upstairs to the sanctuary that was filled with people praising God. The anointing was so thick you could cut it with a knife. There at the front of the church leading everyone in praising God was a six-foot tall redheaded woman. Her name was Vickie Walber.

We were new Christians and a new couple, and we watched in amazement as the Spirit of God moved through this handmaiden as she preached about relationship with God in boldness, authority, and power. When she prayed for the people, they were slain in the Spirit and would fall to the ground. Many got up healed and delivered and set free.

My wife Nicole and myself were both healed of chlamydia, and I was healed of a hiatal hernia. I witnessed people who were healed from cancer, deafness, blindness, and infirmities. Many were delivered from demons and even the dead were raised to life. Multitudes of others were giving their hearts to Jesus and being filled with the Holy Ghost under her ministry.

Vickie Walber performed our wedding ... and this was just the beginning. The attending on my side were all heathens and on Nicole's side were mostly Mormon. The power of God showed up and shook everyone in the place. It was reported to be one of the most awesome weddings they ever attended.

I could write a book about the things God has done through this handmaiden. She is generous, courageous, bold, and loved by God and us.

John

I met Vickie Walber in 1989. I was 18 at the time. We were led to visit a church in Anchorage, Alaska, that she and her sister had started.

I experienced the power of God the moment I entered the sanctuary, and although I was new to church life, I recognized the authority and bold truth of the gospel being preached by this handmaiden of the Lord.

After attending a few services, I received a word from God telling me, "This is where I have planted you, and this is where you will grow."

I am 53 now as I write these things, but the revival I experienced as a teenager through her ministry still remains in the hearts of the people today.

She has been a spiritual mother, mentor, trainer, and friend to me and to thousands of people all over the world.

God has used her to lead multitudes to the Lord. In the church, she emphasized having the reverent fear of God and letting the Holy Spirit have his way, which through the years has led to many miracles, signs, and wonders.

The blind see, the deaf hear, the lame walk, and the dead have been raised – Glory to God!

She is one of the most generous and genuine people I know. She has dedicated her time, her resources, and her life to helping others and furthering the Kingdom of God.

Luanne

"Therefore, if anyone is in Christ, the new creation has come: The old has gone, the new is here!" (2 Corinthians 5:17). It's not enough to know about Jesus. The adversary knows about Him, too. When I made the decision to truly know Jesus, to develop a friendship with Him, to embrace a holy mentorship, everything changed. This is when He sent Vickie into my life.

I came to realize my life was not my own. I had to cast off my old ways of thinking and start doing things differently in an effort to start reconciling myself to Him. Every person making that decision becomes a new creation, not merely improved or reformed, but truly transformed. Life looks—and is—completely different.

We begin to see His Creation with new eyes; we are given a heart of compassion. We don't just ignore sin, we avoid it. There is a big difference between continuing to sin and continuing to live in sin. It's impossible to reach sinless perfection in this life; however, the redeemed Christian is being sanctified day by day, sinning less and less and truly cringing each time we miss the mark. After all, we are now freed from sin, and it no longer has power over us. (Romans 6:6-7)

Vickie baptized me in His Holy Spirit, and I began walking in the fruit of His Holy Spirit which is 'love, joy, peace, longsuffering (having or showing patience in spite of troubles), kindness, goodness, faithfulness, gentleness, self-control' (Galatians 5:22-23); I also learned how to walk in the awesome Power of our Most High God with His precious gifts to us:

There are different kinds of gifts.
But it is the same Holy Spirit Who gives them.
There are different kinds of work to be done for Him.
But the work is for the same Lord.
There are different ways of doing His work.
But it is the same God who uses all these ways in all people.
The Holy Spirit works in each person in one way or another for the good of all.
One person is given the gift of teaching words of wisdom.
Another person is given the gift of teaching what he has learned and knows.

These gifts are by the same Holy Spirit.
One person receives the gift of faith.
Another person receives the gifts of healing.
These gifts are given by the same Holy Spirit.
One person is given the gift of doing powerful works.
Another person is given the gift of speaking God's Word.
Another person is given the gift of telling the difference
between the Holy Spirit and false spirits.
Another person is given the gift of speaking in special sounds.
Another person is given the gift of telling what these special sounds
mean.
But it is the same Holy Spirit, the Spirit of God,
Who does all these things. He gives to each person as He wants to give.
1 Corinthians 12:4-11

Jesus said to them, "Go into all the world and preach the gospel to all creation. Whoever believes and is baptized will be saved, but whoever does not believe will be condemned. And these signs will accompany those who believe: In my name they will drive out demons; they will speak in new tongues; they will pick up snakes with their hands; and when they drink deadly poison, it will not hurt them at all; they will place their hands on sick people, and they will get well" (Mark 16:15-18).

Vickie taught me these things. As a willing vessel of God, she showed me all of this through the love of His Powerful Spirit. I have experienced miracles and healings. I have laid hands on others and watched in awe as our Lord God healed them! I have witnessed miracles firsthand, including two men brought back to life from certain death.

Together with our brothers and sisters saved by Jesus Christ and baptized in His Holy Spirit, we work toward being in constant union with Him for His glory and our good. We study the Bible, meditate on it, study and talk with one another about His Word, and seek clarity from Him.

The more we learn about Him from His Word, and pray, the more God works in our lives. We begin to produce in us what God intended for us all along. We become more like Him.

Born again in the Spirit, we become aware that our "death" is the end of our old sinful nature which was nailed to the cross with Christ. It was buried with Him, and just as He was raised up by the Father, so are we raised up to "walk in newness of life" (Romans 6:4).

That old me had to die, Lord Jesus.
You knew it, I knew it.
Thank you for pulling me out of the mess I made
of the life you gave me.
Thank You for another chance.
Thank You for bringing Vickie Walber into my life,
best teacher, beloved friend, and precious sister
forever through You.
Amen

"I live prepared.

The greatest Miracle I've ever seen

is watching men and women giving their hearts to God.

You have heaven on your side.

All creation is now moving for you.

You don't look like other people.

You don't dress like other people.

He doesn't care what you wear.

He sees your heart.

For Your Glory and the building of Your Kingdom."

~ Vickie Walber

Prophetic Word to Vickie

I Clean From the Inside Out, Not the Outside In

You cannot walk by appearance only

For a changed heart will make for a changed life

The things that used to be will be no more

Allow Me to do the work that I have been sent to do

In your hearts and in your minds, in your souls and in your Spirit

I chose you, you did not choose Me

And the way seems hard for a time, but only because you don't let go

I can bless you in your mistakes

I can advance you in your own little kingdom

For My eye is on everything

And My hand is on everything

Not just some things but all things

I know when a sparrow falls, every hair on your head

Do you think I do not know the opposition in your life

If you would just let go inside

Inside, and it will manifest itself on the outside

Out of the abundance of the heart not only do you speak but you live

You move and you have your being; so allow Me in all the way

Not to just some of the way, I want all the way

For David was a man after mine own heart, yet he made mistakes

I never turned my back on him, I never sat him down

He remained King and fulfilled what I wanted him to do

That's all I'm asking as you would fill the things I desire for you to do

For a way may seem right to a person, but the way there is death

So choose this day whom you are going to serve

Did I not send you the Holy Ghost on the day of Pentecost

He is still hovering over your head, waiting to perform the will of My

Son

Don't doubt or disbelieve, Faith is an action

Faith goes deep in all mankind

But it's where you choose to use your faith that matters to Me

Put Me first, put Me first

For I am a jealous God, and I love you with a longing you will never

understand

Until we stand face to face

Put those things aside that so easily beset you

They're not necessary, you have no axe to grind, no things to prove

For we all live under the shadow of the most high God whether

We are in or out of His kingdom, it rains on the just and the unjust

And the sun shines on the just and the unjust, but yet my children will

be different

My children will walk in victory, even in their own lives, do not regret

your choices

I'll train you through them, do not regret your mistakes, I will train

you through them

Know and understand I am the living God who formed and hewn you

in your mother's womb

I knew you before the foundations of the world

Let Me be who I am, so you can be who you are

Thus sayeth the Lord

Vickie wants her last words on earth to be:

"Bring them into Your Kingdom, Lord."

ENDNOTES

[1] Crawford, Polly. *Angel of the Flesh.* 2012. (Create Space Publishing: North Charleston, South Carolina) pp. 22-23.

[2] Crawford, Polly. *Angel of the Flesh.* 2012. (Create Space Publishing: North Charleston, South Carolina) pp. 120-121.

[3] Crawford, Polly. *Angel of the Flesh.* 2012. (Create Space Publishing: North Charleston, South Carolina)

[4] Crawford, Polly. *Angel of the Flesh.* 2012. (Create Space Publishing: North Charleston, South Carolina)

[5] Trombley, Charles. *Who Said Women Can't Teach?* 1985. (Bridge-Logos: Alachua, Florida) pp. 53-54.

[6] Trombley, Charles. *Who Said Women Can't Teach?* 1985. (Bridge-Logos: Alachua, Florida) pp. 266-267.

[7] Nelson, Luanne. *Daring to Believe: You Have Unopened Presents With Your Name Written on Them.* 2021. (Nico 11 Publishing & Design: Mukwonago, Wisconsin) pp. 74-76.

[8] From: https://www.jonasclark.com/revolutionary-review/christian-living-and-spiritual-growth/how-to-recognize-the-characteristics-of-a-religious-spirit

[9] From: https://www.christianwebsite.com/what-did-jesus-say-about-church

ABOUT THE AUTHOR

Dr. Luanne Nelson

Dr. Luanne Nelson is a Chaplain, Biblical Counselor, Street Minister and Best-Selling Author.

She authored *Daring to Believe – You Have Unopened Presents With Your Name Written on Them*, filled with testimonies of modern-day miracles. *Madness, Mayhem and Modern Medicine – How in God's Creation Did We Get Here, and What Do We Do Now?* offers a biblical perspective of the challenges we are facing in the world today.

Flipping Tables, The Seven Deadly Sins and Stories of Redemption, is a study in God's grace and deliverance, containing a collection of stories from several people who have had powerful first-hand encounters with the mercy and love of Jesus.

As a co-author, Dr. Nelson's contributions can be found in several books including *Comfort for the Grieving, Holy Whole and Fit,* and *A Few Words on Your Identity in Christ.* Her heartfelt musings are featured in *The Miracle Effect, The Breakthrough Effect,* and *The Identity Effect* presented by FEW International Publications. She was invited to add a chapter about "Aging Gracefully," in the Amazon #1 New Release 2019 edition of *Natural & Organic Healing: Your Ultimate Guide to Health & Wellness.*

For more information, please visit her website: www.LuanneNelson.com

And we know that all things work together
for good to those who love God,
to those who are called according to His *purpose.*
Romans 8:28